INSIDE OUT

Inside Out

Selected Poetry & Translations

ALASTAIR REID

Introduction by Douglas Dunn

First published in Great Britain in 2008
by Polygon, an imprint of Birlinn Ltd
West Newington House
10 Newington Road
Edinburgh eh9 1qs

9   8   7   6   5   4   3   2   1

www.birlinn.co.uk

ISBN   978 1 84697 069 6

British Library Cataloguing-in-Publication Data
A catalogue record for this book is available
on request from the British Library.

Typeset in Great Britain by Antony Gray
Printed and bound by Cromwell Press Ltd, Trowbridge, Wiltshire

This time for Ian and Ella

Contents

POETRY (*continued*)

WRITERS

ON TRANSLATION

SELECTED TRANSLATIONS
Jorge Luis Borges

CONTENTS

Pablo Neruda

José Emilio Pacheco

Heberto Padilla

Eugenio Montejo

Enrique Lihn

Alvaro Mutis

ACKNOWLEDGEMENTS
page 281

Introduction

'Amazement is the thing.'

For many years Alastair Reid could hardly be said to have been a presence in Scottish poetry. No one need search too hard for a reason – he simply wasn't here, but in the US.A, France, Switzerland, Spain, or elsewhere in the Hispanic world. He appeared in some Scottish anthologies, but early in his career he seems to have been drawn towards what he has called 'a deliberate, chosen strangeness', that is, as opposed to deracination, an 'otherness' which some Scots have found irresistible, the prime examples being Robert Louis Stevenson for whom Scotland was 'that blessed, beastly place', and Muriel Spark who saw herself as of 'Scottish formation'.

Roots are portable enough for a poet or any sort of writer either to eat them for breakfast, forget them, or be reminded through overhearing an accent or noticing a coincidence in the weather. In Scotland the temptation has been to make too much of them. Nationality sometimes seems scattered all over the page, a superficial squandering, an anxiety rather than a poetic fascination. For much of the time Reid is a poet of specific places rather than his nationality, a choice, or identity, which he shares with Norman MacCaig. In any case, a poet's places (and events, memories, loves) are remade by imagination whatever the immediacy of their origins in reality.

Reid is well aware of the continuities and vulnerabilities of poetry. 'Poem Without Ends', for example, opens:

> One cannot take the beginning out of the air
> Saying 'It is the time: the hour is here'.
> The process is continuous as wind, . . .

Meditating on these lines encourages me to believe that one of the ways Reid differs from most Scottish poets of around his age is more than an openness to experience of the world, but an unwillingness to see a poem as a closed or finished artefact. Or, as Paul Valéry believed, a poem is never finished, merely abandoned. Another way of putting it is to cite what a friend of mine used to call 'the miraculous school of poetry', poems, that is, ought to happen because they must: the poet didn't choose to write them, but was compelled. It's not a recipe for artless spontaneity, but its resourceful opposite. Reid's artistry in language is conspicuous, in both poetry and prose; his command of cadence, phrase, image, and narrative, is robust, or delicate when it needs to be. Yet in a brief introductory note in *Weathering* (1978) he claimed the book was 'something of a farewell on my part to formal poetry, which seems to me now something of an artificial gesture, like wearing a tie'. It read then as too bad to be true; and it still puzzles me. 'I am more interested in the essential act of putting-well-into-words, good writing.'

When asked why he didn't seem to have written a poem in a long while, Philip Larkin liked to say, 'You can't write a poem unless you've a poem to write.' Could something similar have happened to Alastair Reid and he had the sense and courage to recognise that his poetry was finished? Of course, you can always change your mind, either back to what it was before, or take a different tack entirely. Reid, though, has the comforts of translation, and prose. New poems may be few and far between, but he is still the same eminent man of letters, and wise in his art.

Poetry has its mysteries as Alastair Reid acknowledges on virtually every page. Where they come from, those unpredictable accuracies of seeing, imagining, remembering, and saying, is, if not exactly anyone's guess, then bordering on the secret; and an attentive reader's answer is often likely to be wrong. Take, for example, the third stanza of 'The Waterglass':

> An underwater wind
> ruffled the red-roofed shallows
> where wading stilt-legged children
> stood in the clouded sand,
> and down from the knee-deep harbour
> a ladder led to the drowned.

Evocative as these lines are of a boy, or man, using a glass-bottomed box to look at the coastal sea bed, their perceptiveness, and that of the poem as a whole, goes beyond a memory of what was observed. It enters a realm at once unsettling but filled with a sense of wonder. Some cadences and phrasings are reminiscent of Dylan Thomas when he was being lucid, which is perhaps more obvious at the beginning of 'Isle of Arran':

> Where no one was was where my world was stilled
> into hills that hung behind the lasting water, . . .

Here the mystery arises from asking ourselves where 'lasting' came from – except that water is permanent, and few other phenomena more so in a northern, wet, temperate climate. That makes 'lasting' no less surprising an epithet; and one of the ways in which poetry happens is when surprise coincides with a reader's recognition, or leads to understanding anew aspects of life and the world of which the reader was ignorant or only half-aware.

'James Bottle's Year' uses a calendar form with a tightness of sound achieved through a deceptively off-hand use of rhyme. Rarely, if ever, has Reid been the all-out tie-wearing formalist he dismissed thirty years ago in his remarks in *Weathering*. Instead, his metrical astuteness avoids any taint of showing off and opts for an appropriate form. The simplicity of the month-by-month structure of 'James Bottle's Year' contributes to its success as a portrait of a mythical or iconic countryman, perhaps a poacher, or gamekeeper, or agricultural worker, though more as an emblem of hard life. Setting and chronology seem Scottish, maybe Galloway; but that might not be so, and I could be misled by memories of books by John McNeillie and Ian Niall. As with many of Reid's poems, its place and events are simultaneously local and universal.

Like Stevenson, and many before and since, Reid appears to have loved maps, charts, atlases and islands. Certainly the way he describes them in 'Directions for a Map' suggests an ingrained affection as well as an awareness of the knowledge they do not disclose:

Crossing the threads of roads to nibbled coastlines,
the rivers run in veins that crack the surface.
Mountains are dark like hair, and here and there
lakes gape like moth holes with the sea showing through.

Between the seaports stutter dotted shiplines,
crossing designs of latitude and language.
The towns are flying names. The sea is titled.
A compass crowns the corner like a seal.

But, 'There are no signs for love or trouble'.

And even though, on any printed landscape,
directions never tell you where to go,
maps are an evening comfort to the traveller –
a pencil line will quickly take him home.

Too much could be made of Reid's itinerancy, just as a critic could
overdo sniffing for the fragrance of influences (Auden, for example,
in 'Directions for a Map'). Good poems are seldom the result of a
flying visit. 'New Hampshire' (Robert Frost country) reads as a
well-experienced poem, as do 'Maine Coast', 'Chelsea Reach' and
'Geneva'. He likes to settle in first, then leave. As he writes in 'The
Spiral':

Places, addresses, faces left behind.
The present is a devious wind
obliterating days and promises.
Tomorrow is a tinker's guess.
Marooned in cities, dreaming of greenness,
or dazed by journeys, dreading to arrive –
change, change is where I live.

It is more profound, more thoughtful, than 'love them and leave
them', whether applied to places or lovers.
   Curiosity ranks high in Reid's mind and range of choices.

Face it. Curiosity
will not cause us to die
only lack of it will.

> Never to want to see
> the other side of the hill
> of that improbable country
> where living is an idyll
> (although a probable hell)
> would kill us all.
> Only the curious
> have if they live a tale
> worth telling at all.

Two other cat poems, 'Propinquity' and 'Cat-Faith', when added to 'Curiosity', appear to create Reid's persona as a nocturnal cat-man:

> When, libertine at dark,
> we let the visions in, and the black window
> grotesques us back, our world unbalances.

Feline monstrousness is redeemed by gestures of respectability:

> Yet, to endure that unknown night by night,
> must we not be sure, with cat-insight,
> we can afford its terrors, and that full day
> will find us at the desk, sane, unafraid –
> cheeks shaven, letters written, bills paid?

'Mediterranean' is more than a poem that tries to live up to its title. Embedded in it is a discreetly but passionately expressed love poem. It reads as a poem conveying a feeling of love as transient. 'The garden is not ours' is repeated twice, the first time at the end of the first stanza, and then as the last line of the poem:

> Dear one, this present Eden
> lays down its own condition:
> we should not ask to wait.
> No angel drives us out,
> but time, without a word,
> will show among the flowers,
> sure as a flaming sword.
> The garden is not ours.

When he writes about love there is an active presence of privacy. Nothing is hidden. Instead, it's made over into fiction, as if writing in your own language is a way of 'translating' experiences and feelings into it. He enjoyed a close association with Robert Graves on Mallorca from 1956 to 1961. Towards the end Reid fell in love with Graves's current muse, with whom he eloped. The episode is described in his affectionate memoir of Graves, and, with considerable bile, in Martin Seymour-Smith's biography of 1982. (Acolytes of the same elder poet seldom have anything good to say of each other.) But that privacy was always there, and hardly to be explained by his affair with Margot Callas. There could be a Gravesian scenario in 'A Lesson for Beautiful Women' – 'six eyes', 'three goddesses' &c. At the same time that sort of speculation leaves a bad taste in the mouth and overstates biography's place in criticism.

Diversity is what Reid may have learned from his many conversations with Graves and close proximity to Graves's example as a writer – poetry, prose and 'the alchemy of translation'. But whereas Graves translated mainly from ancient texts, Reid has translated modern Hispanic and Ibero-American poetry. Reid was unimpressed by the University of St Andrews which he attended in 1946–50 after war service in the Royal Navy, as he makes clear in two poems, 'The Academy' and 'The O-Filler'. Disdain for academies and academics never did a poet any harm, though, while, for a translator of poetry it is surely more important that the poet-translator find an affinity with the translated. In his essay 'Fictions', Reid tells us that he first met Jorge Luis Borges in 1964 when Borges had already succumbed to hereditary blindness.

> I found at once a coincidence of mind, not simply an enthusiasm for his writings, but more, a complete accord with the view of language implied in all his writing. . . . Borges referred to all his writings – essays, stories, poems, reviews – as fictions.

Some might find it odd or ironic that the anti-bookish Alastair Reid should translate the inveterately bookish Borges, Director of the National Library of Argentina, whose life and mind were devoted to books and submerged in them, and in dreams of them:

Care of this city of books he handed over
to sightless eyes, which now can do no more
than read in libraries of dream the poor
and senseless paragraphs that dawns deliver

to wishful scrutiny. In vain the day
squanders on these same eyes its infinite tomes,
as distant as the inaccessible volumes
that perished once in Alexandria.

Only a poet nimble in versification could have achieved these translations of Borges' poems. They read like radiant poems in English, almost a brilliant mimicry in English of a voice in Spanish with an Argentinian history behind it as well as a near-universal erudition. Two factors perhaps made the task just that little bit easier. One, Reid knew Borges and conversed at length with him. And two, Borges' affection for and knowledge of Anglo-Saxon and Nordic culture.

When one poet translates another, perhaps superior, almost always different, he or she is performing an act of homage that seeks for an elusive accuracy. Part of the business of translation is simply to make poems available to those who do not understand the original language. While that was conceded by the great critic Walter Benjamin, in his 'The Task of the Translator', he also claimed that translation was 'a mode of its own'. That is, he believed that 'the task of the translator, too, may be regarded as distinct and clearly differentiated from the task of the poet'. For Benjamin, 'The intention of the poet is spontaneous, primary, graphic; that of the translator is derivative, ultimate, ideational'. But what if the translator *is* a poet, and a good poet at that, rather that *artifex additus artifici*, an 'added artificer'? This is where poetic translation becomes interesting and aesthetically challenging; it becomes as creative as writing an original poem.

In 'An ABC of Translating Poetry', appended to his *The Poetics of Translation* (1993), Willis Barnstone writes:

Translation is an art BETWEEN tongues, and the child born of the art lives forever BETWEEN home and alien city. Once across the border, in new garb, the orphan remembers or conceals the old town, and appears new-born and different.

Moving BETWEEN tongues, translation acquires difference. Because the words and grammar of each language differ from every other language, the transference of a poem from one language to another involves differing sounds and prosody. And because there are no perfect word equivalents between languages or even within the same language (as Borges proves in his story of the mad Menard) perfection in translation is inconceivable.

A translator can accept that readily enough but still be stuck with the problem of what to do with versification and rhyme in original texts when they don't correspond to those of the translator's language. Reid's rhymes in his versions of Borges are happily unforced, natural, opportunistic, while his use of iambic pentameter (the most common line in English) matches Spanish hendecasyllabics.

Some are adept at living in another language. (For others it's to feel constantly like the village idiot.) A poet-translator has to live not just in another language but in its poetry. Translating will also pull you into the life, personality, and convictions of the translated. Both Borges and Neruda were very different from each other and each different from Alastair Reid. Neruda, for example, was a diplomat, communist, and while it is easy to warm to his hedonism it seems awkward in the context of his overarching fervour in the cause of universal social justice. Neruda was aware of the contrast of his love of food and wine with his political commitment, although I doubt if he saw them as tangential. His politics were at the service of 'the justice of eating', as he wrote in 'The great tablecloth'.

> The lamb is gold on its coals
> and the onion undresses.
> It is sad to eat in dinner clothes,
> like eating in a coffin,
> but eating in convents
> is like eating underground.
> Eating alone is a disappointment,

but not eating matters more,
is hollow and green, has thorns
like a chain of fish hooks
trailing from the heart,
clawing at your insides.

. . . Let us sit down soon to eat
with all those who haven't eaten;
let us spread great tablecloths,
put salt in the lakes of the world,
set up planetary bakeries,
tables with strawberries in snow,
and a plate like the moon itself
from which we can all eat.

For now I ask no more
than the justice of eating.

Neruda's startling imagery, his vernacular surrealism delivered on a direct, democratic voice, when introduced in translations also offered new possibilities of writing in English (as well as many other languages).

What does living in another language do to a poet? It could perhaps submerge him in translation, weaken the instinctive and necessary servitude to his or her mother tongue, the language in which a childhood was lived. It could also provide access to stories and images which would otherwise have been unavailable, and extend them to readers and other writers. I believe this could be the case in what might be Reid's most remarkable poem, 'The Tale the Hermit Told'. A masterly dramatic monologue, it is a fiction worthy of Marquez, the story of how a village came to be lost. A boy – who is now, years later, the hermit of the title, and the poem's speaker – is bewitched by a gypsy girl on a day of fiesta.

Time in that moment hung
upside down. In a gulp, I drank the wine.
What happened next? You must listen.
Goggling boys, girls, dogs, band, gypsies, village,
dove, magician, all rolled down my throat.

Even the music glugged once and was gone.
I was standing nowhere, horrified, alone,
waiting for her eyes to appear and laugh
the afternoon back, but nothing moved or happened.
Nothing, nothing, nothing.

And now, as used to be said, read on.

DOUGLAS DUNN, July 2008

POETRY

If we stop pretending for a moment that we were born fully-dressed in a service flat, and remember that we were born stark naked into a pandemonium of most unnatural phenomena, then we know how out-of-place, how lost, how amazed, how miraculous we are. And this reality is the province of poetry.

Christopher Fry

The poems in this volume are those from my earlier books that seem to me to merit a continuing existence. They were most of them written when poetry occupied my whole writing attention. Since then, I have written few poems, but have used whatever I absorbed from writing poems to bring into English the work of some of the Latin American poets I have known and admired.

A. R.

An Instance

Perhaps the accident of a bird
crossing the green window, a simultaneous phrase
of far singing, and a steeplejack
poised on the church spire, changing the gold clock,
set the moment alight. At any rate, a word
in that instant of realising catches fire,
ignites another, and soon the page is ablaze
with a wildfire of writing. The clock chimes in the square.

All afternoon, in a scrawl of time,
the mood still smoulders. Rhyme remembers rhyme,
and words summon the moment when amazement
ran through the senses like a flame.
Later, the song forgotten, the sudden bird
flown who-knows-where, the incendiary word
long since crossed out, the steeplejack gone home,
their moment burns again, restored
to its spontaneity. The poem stays.

Poem Without Ends

One cannot take the beginning out of the air
saying 'It is the time: the hour is here'.
The process is continuous as wind,
the bird observed, not rising, but in flight,
unrealised, in motion in the mind.

The end of everything is similar, never
actually happening, but always over.
The agony, the bent head, only tell
that already in the heart the innocent evening
is thick with all the ferment of farewell.

Once at Piertarvit

Once at Piertarvit,
one day in April,
the edge of spring,
with the air a–ripple
and sea like knitting,
as Avril and Ann
and Ian and I
walked in the wind
along the headland,
Ian threw an apple
high over Piertarvit.

Not a great throw,
you would say, if you'd seen it,
but good for Ian.
His body tautened,
his arm let go
like a flesh-and-bone bow,

and the hard brown apple
left over from autumn
flew up and up,
crossing our gaze,
from the cliff at Piertarvit.

Then all at once, horror
glanced off our eyes,
Ann's, mine, Avril's.
As the apple curved
in the stippled sky,
at the top of its arc,
it suddenly struck
the shape of a bird,
a gull that had glided
down from nowhere
above Piertarvit.

We imagined the thud
and the thin ribs breaking,
blood, and the bird
hurtling downwards.
No such thing.
The broad wings wavered
a moment only,
then air sustained them.
The gull glided on
while the apple fell
in the sea at Piertarvit.

Nobody spoke.
Nobody whistled.
In that one moment,
our world had shifted.
The four of us stood
stock-still with awe
till, breaking the spell,
Ian walked away

with a whirl in his head.
The whole sky curdled
over Piertarvit.

I followed slowly,
with Ann and Avril
trailing behind.
We had lost our lightness.
Even today,
old as I am,
I find it hard
to say, without wonder,
'Ian hit a bird
with an apple, in April,
once at Piertarvit.'

Wishes

Sudden silence, an angel passing over,
two saying the same word, simultaneously,
a star falling, the first fruit of the year,
the breastbone of the chicken, scraped and dry –
each an occasion to wish on, a wish given.

Easy enough for children, for whom to wish
is only a way of bringing a party closer
or acquiring pennies or cake, and for whose sake
we attend to teeth beneath stones and believe in magic,
not indulgently but somehow because
each time the silver coin appears where the tooth was,
the party seems quick in coming, and beggars ride
pell-mell over the countryside.

But for ourselves, with fewer teeth and no faith
in miracles or good angels, a falling star
is likely to be uncomfortable. Oh, we can ask for
new lives, more money, or a change of face,
but hardly seriously. The heart is lacking.
We know too much, and wishing smacks of daydream
and discontent – not magic. Anyway, we are wary
of strings and snags or, worse, that, once fulfilled,
the thing we wished for might be old and cold.

Yet still the children come, with serious
rapt faces, offering us wishes.
Take this wishbone, delicate where the breast was,
whitened now by the sun, stick-brittle.
Hold one stem of it, lightly, with your little
finger. I will hold the other.
Now make your wish, my love; but never tell.

And I? I always wish you well;
but here, in this poise before the fruit can fall,
or the star burn out, or the word dwindle,
before the hovering angel
flies out of mind, before the bone is broken,
I wish we wish the same wish, the unspoken.

Was, Is, Will Be

It was to have been
an enchanted spring –
the house friendly,
the neighbours kindly,
the mornings misted,
the birds soft-breasted,
the children easy,
the days lazy
with early flowers,
the time, ours.

Not as it is –
days ill-at-ease,
a plague of crows,
the first leaves slow,
the children jumpy,
the cook skimpy,
slant rain in streams,
goblin dreams,
the roof leaky,
work unlikely.

Or will be later
when, like a dead letter,
the past stiffens
and afterthought softens.
Yet, distant in winter,
I still will wonder –
was it we who engendered
the spring's condition,
or a ghost we had angered
with expectation?

Frog Dream

Nightlong, frogs in the pool
croak out calamity till, wakeful,
I interpret each crooked syllable.

The sound is churlish, coarse –
frog words grating out a hoarse
chorus of drowned remorse,
as I do, in half-sleep,
until, drifting, I cannot keep
the dark from deepening

or dream voices from becoming
peepers and grunters, churning
my madness over. The pool is lapping,

weed–streaked, in my head.
Frogs echo from the edges of the bed,
in the grieving voices of the long dead,

grudges long hidden in their old throats,
hauntings, water horror, hates.
My fear is a slow crescendo of frog notes . . .
Later, awake in the sanity of dawn,
I walk to the pool, limpid under the sun.
What did I dream? The frogs have all gone down.

The Colour of Herring

I read in the fishbooks that the herring
is black-backed and silver-sided,
is blue-flecked and silver-faceted,
is gray-green shot with silver,
is black and green and silver,
is blue and glass.
I find the herring in my hands
has all the silver of the evening,
all the blue of the bay,
all the green of the deep sea over the side.
The black may easily be in my mood.
The silver certainly flakes my sleeve.
But over my hands in its dying moment spills
the herring's blood
which, silver, green, black, blue aside,
runs unmistakably red.

The Waterglass

A church tower crowned the town,
double in air and water,
and over anchored houses
the round bells rolled at noon.
Bubbles rolled to the surface.
The drowning bells swirled down.

The sun burned in the bay.
A lighthouse towered downward,
moored in mirroring fathoms.
The seaweed swayed its tree.
The boat below me floated
upside down on the sky.

An underwater wind
ruffled the red-roofed shallows
where wading stilt-legged children
stood in the clouded sand,
and down from the knee-deep harbour
a ladder led to the drowned.

Gulls fell out of the day.
The thrown net met its image
in the window of the water.
A ripple slurred the sky.
My hand swam up to meet me,
and I met myself in the sea.

Mirrored, I saw my face
in the underworld of the water,
and saw my drowned self sway in
the glass day underneath –
till I spoke to my speaking likeness,
and the moment broke with my breath.

Isle of Arran

Where no one was was where my world was stilled
into hills that hung behind the lasting water,
a quiet quilt of heather where bees slept,
and a single slow bird in circles winding
round the axis of my head.

Any wind being only my breath, the weather
stopped, and a woollen cloud smothered the sun.
Rust and a mist hung over the clock of the day.
A mountain dreamed in the light of the dark
and marsh mallows were yellow for ever.

Still as a fish in the secret loch alone
I was held in the water where my feet found ground
and the air where my head ended,
all thought a prisoner of the still sense –
till a butterfly drunkenly began the world.

James Bottle's Year

December finds him
outside, looking skyward.
The year gets a swearword.

His rage is never permanent.
By January he's out,
silent and plough-bent.

All white February,
he's in a fury
of wind-grief and ground-worry.

By March, he's back
scouring the ground for luck,
for rabbit-run and deer-track.

April is all sounds and smiles.
The hill is soft with animals.
His arms describe miles.

The local girls say
he's honeyed and bee-headed
at haytime in May.

In June,
he'll stay up late, he'll moon
and talk to children.

No one sees him in July.
At dawn, he'll ride away
with distance in his eye.

In August, you'd assume
yourself to be almost welcome.
He keeps open time.

But, on one September morning,
you'll see cloud-worries form.
His eyes flash storm warnings.

October is difficult.
He tries to puzzle out
If it's his or the season's fault.

In November, he keeps still
through hail and snowfall,
thinking through it all.

What's causing the odd weather?
Himself, or the capricious air?
Or the two together?

December, breathing hard,
he's back outside, hurling skyward
his same swearword.

Directions for a Map

Birds' eyes see almost this, a tiny island
odd as a footprint on a painted sea.
But maps set margins. Here, the land is measured,
changed to a flat, explicit world of names.

Crossing the threads of roads to nibbled coastlines,
the rivers run in veins that crack the surface.
Mountains are dark like hair, and here and there
lakes gape like moth holes with the sea showing through.

Between the seaports stutter dotted shiplines,
crossing designs of latitude and language.
The towns are flying names. The sea is titled.
A compass crowns the corner like a seal.

Distance is spelt in alphabets and numbers.
Arrows occur at intervals of inches.
There are no signs for love or trouble, only
dots for a village and a cross for churches.

Here space is free for once from time and weather.
The sea has pause. To plot is possible.
Given detachment and a careful angle,
all destinations are predictable.

And given, too, the confidence of distance,
strangers may take a hundred mural journeys.
For once the paths are permanent, the colours
outlast the seasons and the deaths of friends.

And even though, on any printed landscape,
directions never tell you where to go,
maps are an evening comfort to the traveller –
a pencil line will quickly take him home.

Scotland

It was a day peculiar to this piece of the planet,
when larks rose on long thin strings of singing
and the air shifted with the shimmer of actual angels.
Greenness entered the body. The grasses
shivered with presences, and sunlight
stayed like a halo on hair and heather and hills.
Walking into town, I saw, in a radiant raincoat,
the woman from the fish-shop. 'What a day it is!'
cried I, like a sunstruck madman.
And what did she have to say for it?
Her brow grew bleak, her ancestors raged in their graves
as she spoke with their ancient misery:
'We'll pay for it, we'll pay for it, we'll pay for it!'

Tiree

Over the walking foreshore cluttered
black with the tide's untidy wrack,
and pools that brimmed with the moon,
I trespassed underwater.
My feet found seabed sand.
The night wore guilt like a watermark
and down the guilty dark,
the gulls muttered to windward.
Far out, the tide spoke back.

Across the morning clean of my walking
ghost and the driftwood litter,
singly I walked into singing light.
The rocks walked light on the water,
and clouds as clean as spinnakers
puffed in the sea-blue sky.
A starfish signed the sand. Beyond,
I faced the innocent sea.

New Hampshire

Here, green has grown to be a habit.
The hills are forest-headed, not for farmers.
Trees hug the land as close as fur.
A lake looks naked. There is no way in,

except for local animals. And the roads
stumble and lurch down humps of stubbled dust.
Flowers bloom at ease without being told
and grass has grown untidily, in a hurry.

Here, the tall elm and the leaking maple,
and apple trees as gnarled as farmers' knuckles
ooze stickily with sap or syrup.
Forests are tumbled to make room for trees.

Houses are hewn and hidden in the hedges,
all pine and wooden pegs. The paths are lost.
Towns are a pilgrimage away.
Here, families live alone in hand-made homes.

Only the animals are seasoned owners.
The lakes belong to frogs with broken voices.
Farms are inhabited by rabbits.
A fox barks like a landlord down the dark.

Deer have been known to tiptoe down for apples.
A snake may suddenly scribble out of sight.
Your eyes are never sure. Each evening
someone comes back from almost seeing a bear.

Here, space is sweet with extra air. The silence
is positive, and has a steady sound.
You seem to own the woods, until
a shotgun coughs, to warn you, in the valley.

A week is a whole anthology of weather.
The country has you somehow at its mercy.
The size of the moon begins to matter,
and every night a whippoorwill leaves omens.

All names are hung on stilted mailboxes,
spasmodically fed with last week's letters.
The children quickly learn to wave.
A summer changes strangers into neighbours.

Here, one is grateful to the tolerant landscape,
and glad to be known by men with leather faces
who welcome anything but questions.
Words, like the water, must be used with care.

Maine Coast

These islands are all anchored deep dark down.
Pines pitch-thick, gnarled green, and rich of root,
logs lying, lopped boughs, branches, broken rock,
the bow of a boat, the length of a life, weed-water.
I am an island, this is nearest home.

Time is called morning, clinging moist, mist-ridden.
Days are disguised, the houses are half trees –
wind in the attic, sea in the cellar, words
all alien. Though sun burns books, blinds eyes.
I see through to the bone and the beginning.

Tomorrow waits for the net; today tells
time in circles on the trunks, in tides.
Boats are lucky, love is lucky, children
are kings – and we must listen to the wise
wind saying all our other lives are lies.

Galilea

Bleached white, bedazzled
by the bright light falling,
the hilltop holds me up.
Below, the coastline bares its teeth.

Winded, burned to the bone, between
the stony green of the olive,
the gray grimace of stone,
I look dazedly down.

How to come to rest
in this raw, whittled landscape
where earth, air, fire, and water
bluntly demand obeisance?

Perhaps to fix one place
in a shifting world where time
talks and where too many selves
criss-cross and demand
enactment and re-enactment,

somewhere decent to die in,
somewhere which could become
landscape and vocabulary,
equilibrium, home.

Isla Negra, Chile

Sitting with the Pacific between my toes
in Chile, which I only knew by name,
in Isla Negra, which is not an island,
I listen across amazement to a girl
punctuating the air on a guitar.

There are places too well known to notice
and places unimaginable like dreams.
I am
suspended between the two. I know the sun
of old. I know the sea, over and over,
and once again. I do not know the girl
except by touch. The moment has no name.
After three playings, I will know the tune.

Chelsea Reach

The boat rides watertight, moored, fog-shrouded.
The boy reads, floats, daydreams.
With less daylight, I get to know darkness.

Rueful winter, laying gloom on the river.
Unkind winter, contradictor of comfort.
Blank winter, an unmarked blackboard.

Evenings aboard are longer, with more remembering.
Conclusions break, a long slow march of thought.
I sit in the lamp's pool, my head in darkness.

The boy mutters lost words, the phrases of dreams.
The tide laps him to sleep, nudges him with morning.
He rises, born and beginning. To watch him is wonder.

That might be enough, the hollow hull–shelter
shrouded in winter, shipshape on the river,
the boy bright with questions, I fathering answer

but for the gathering gloom, the looming winter,
the present light breaking, change making fear,
tide on gray tide, another, another, another.

Geneva

In this town, in the blurred and snowy dawn,
under humped eaves, in a lopsided house
built, it would seem, by gnomes, in the first
hushed snowlight, in the snowy hush,
an alarm clock catches and trills time on its tongue
like a clockwork rooster. Silence. And then another

begins to burr in the attic, its small bell
nibbling at the edges of awareness.
So the day speaks. Sleep is left like fallen snow
on the tumbled snow-white bed in which we wake.
And then the bells begin their wrangling preamble
to the hour, giving tongue, tumbling
one over the other, faltering, failing, falling
like snow on the white pillow. Their gold tongues wag
with time. (They are rung, it would seem, by gnomes).
Now, in the town, the day is on its way.
Snowfalls nibble at the windows. In the great
assembly halls, bells ring
along the marble lobbies, calling the delegates in
to the long tables, of words where, crouched
like watchmakers, they worry away
the agendas of the world, their tongues ticking
like mechanisms, and in the earphones
the voices of interpreters trill their small alarms.
Time, gentlemen. Time is what they are telling.
The snow melts silently, the watchsprings twitter.
What was the question? Bells
telling time obscure the answer.
(The clocks never need translation.)
Eyes on the snow, we listen.
The words roll on like bells
marking time; they fall and drift like snow,
leaving their meaning in a watery
residue. The diplomats pace the halls,
watching the clock, attentive to alarms.
All these words telling time fall thick as snowflakes.
We hope for a conclusion from the clock,
which never comes, except in intervals
of snowy silence. Clocks obscure our time.
Now, in the town, something is ticking away.
(Gnomes can be glimpsed at night, in pools of lamplight,
peering through glass at something small and precious,
ticking, and probably gold.)

In this town of telling, we grow old
in a tumble of bells, and over us all
in the continuum
time falls, snow falls, words fall.

The Manse

The house that shored my childhood up
razed to the ground? I stood, amazed,
gawking at a block of air,
unremarkable except
I had hung it once with crazy
daywish and nightmare.

Expecting to pass a wistful
indulgent morning, I had sprung the gate.
Facing me was a wood
between which and myself
a whole crow-gabled and slated
mythology should have stood.

No room now for the rambling
wry remembering I had planned;
nor could I replant
that plot with a second childhood.
Luck, to have been handed
instead a forgettable element,

and not to have had to meet
regretful ghosts in rooms of glass.
That house by now is fairytale
and I can gloss it over
as easily as passing
clear through a wall.

Mediterranean

However gracefully
the spare leaves of the fig tree
abundant overhead
with native courtesy
include us in their shade,
among the rented flowers
we keep a tenant's station.
The garden is not ours.

Under the arching trellis
the gardener moves below.
Observe him on his knees
with offering of water
for roots that are not his
tendering to a power
whose name he does not know,
but whom he must appease.

So do we too accord
the windings of the vine
and swelling of the olive
a serious mute oblation
and a respectful word,
aware of having put,
in spite of cultivation,
the worm within the fruit.

This garden tenancy
tests our habitual eye.
Now, water and the moon
join what we do not own.
The rent is paid in breath,
and so we freely give
the apple tree beneath
our unpossessive love.

Dear one, this present Eden
lays down its own condition:
we should not ask to wait.
No angel drives us out,
but time, without a word,
will show among the flowers,
sure as a flaming sword.
The garden is not ours.

The Rain in Spain

Unmediterranean
today, the punctual sun
sulks and stays in

and heavily down the mountain
across olive and pine
rolls a scrim of rain.

Faces press to windows.
Strangers moon and booze.
Innkeepers doze.

Slow lopsided clocks
tick away weeks.
Rudely the weather knocks

and starts up old ills,
insect-itch, boils.
The mail brings bills.

Lovers in their houses
quarrel and make promises
or, restless, dream of cities.

Ghosts in the rafters mutter.
Goats grunt and clatter.
Birds augur water.

The Swiss poet is sick.
The postman kicks his dog.
Death overtakes a pig.

Books turn damp and sour.
Thunder grumbles somewhere.
Sleepers groan in nightmare,

each sure that the sky teems
with his personal phantoms,
each doomed to his own bad dreams.

For who is weather-wise
enough to recognise
which ills are the day's, which his?

The Tale the Hermit Told

It was one afternoon when I was young
in a village near here, which no one now remembers –
why, I will tell you – an afternoon of fiesta,
with the bells of the hermitage echoing in the mountains,
and a buzz of voices, and dogs barking. Some said
it could all be heard as far as Calatayud.
I was a boy then, though at that perilous point
when tiny things could terrify and amaze me.
The dust in the village square had been watered down,
and we waited, laughing and jostling
the satin rumps of the gypsy dancers.
Across from us, the girls, all lace and frills,
fluttered like tissue paper. Then at a signal,
as the charcoal-burner's dog rolled over and over,
shedding its ribbons, the village band
blundered into tune, and the day began.
  The dancing dizzied me. There was one gypsy
unlike the others, tall, who spun on her feet,
laughing to herself, lost in her own amazement.
I watched her as though in a dream. All round,
my uncles and other men were calling *olé*
while the women tittered and pouted.
There were more feet than shoes, more wine than glasses,
and more kisses than lips. The sun was burning.
Next came a magician, an ugly sly-eyed man
not from our district. 'Fiesta, fiesta' he called,
then, chanting a kind of spell, he swore
he would conjure a live dove out of the air.
I saw the dove's wing peeping from his pocket,
so I wandered away, hating the sound of him,
among the tables, heavy with food and wine.
And there was the gypsy girl, standing alone,
head turned away to listen, as though she heard

bells in the hills. She saw me, and her eyes,
which were azure, not black, mocked me.
I could not stop looking. Lightly she danced across
and, keeping her eyes on mine, poured out
a glass of golden wine, and put it before me.

    I glanced from her eyes to the wine. In it, the sun
was a small gold coin, the people looked like nuts.
The band were brass buttons, the towering mountains
the size of pebbles, the houses matchboxes
about the thumbnail square. A miniature magician
was letting loose a dove, which floated upwards,
and there, in that golden, glass-held afternoon,
were those mocking eyes. Time in that moment hung
upside down. In a gulp, I drank the wine.

    What happened next? You must listen.
Goggling boys, girls, dogs, band, gypsies, village,
dove, magician, all rolled down my throat.
Even the music glugged once and was gone.
I was standing nowhere, horrified, alone,
waiting for her eyes to appear and laugh
the afternoon back, but nothing moved or happened.
Nothing, nothing, nothing.

    All that night, I lay in a clump of pines
and seemed to hear the hunters with their dogs
(unribboned now) closing to flush me out.
I hid my face in the needles. All the next day,
I tried to wish the village back, to vomit
the wine, to free the white dove and the music.
I could not. And as time passed,
I lived on bitter nuts and bark and grasses,
and grew used to the woods. I am still here
on this barren mountainside. The years are nothing.

    Yet I am sure of this –
that somewhere in my body there is fiesta,
with ribboned dogs, balloons, and children dancing
in a lost village, that only I remember.
Often I have visions, and I hear

voices I know call out. Was it the false magician
who tempted me to magic? Or was it
the gypsy girl who dropped her eyes in a glass
and asked me to work wonders?
Even now, in age, I wait to see her,
still a girl, come spiralling through the woods,
bringing her mystery to me, and with her eyes
teaching me to undream myself, and be
a boy again, believing in a dove
made out of air, that circles overhead
on a lost afternoon of fiesta.

A Game of Glass

I do not believe this room
with its cat and its chandelier,
its chessboard-tiled floor,
its shutters that open out
on an angel playing a fountain,
and the striped light slivering in
to a room that looks the same
in the mirror over my shoulder,
with a second glass-eyed cat.

My book does not look real.
The room and the mirror seem
to be playing a waiting game.
The cat has made its move,
the fountain has one to play,
and the thousand eyes of the angel
in the chandelier above
gleam beadily, and say
the next move is up to me.

How can I trust my luck?
Whatever way I look,
I cannot tell which is the door,
and I do not know who is who –
the thin man in the mirror
or the watery one in the fountain.
The cat is eyeing my book.
What am I meant to do?
Which side is the mirror on?

L'Amour de Moi

The tune at first is odd, though still familiar.
It asks and answers, as you hear
the children playing it on their thin recorders
over and over in the afternoon,
through breath and error, with the huge blue day
hovering overhead. The house dozes,
and guests asleep – uncles, grandmothers, cousins –
accept it easily into their dreams,
like variations on the same cool breeze,
and sigh. The notes, frail moths among the roses,
falter but never fail. A wind passes,
and then the tune again, the first phrase firm,
the second wavering and fanciful,
the last settling, as the air falls still.

Later, at night, its counterpoint –
the family after dinner, lifting down
instruments from the walls, and their huge shadows
huddled, bending together, as candle flames
waver with the first enquiring chord.
Sisters, sweethearts, friends, they yield to the air,
subscribed by lifting strings and the bland oboe,
gloom of the cello, thump of drum.

The children turn in sleep upstairs, dreaming
in waves that widen from their own small music –
heartbeat and breath, the fanciful lift of fiddles,
the falling arm, the last cool phrase, falling.
Shadows pause in their place. Outside,
the garden breathes beneath suspended stars.

This is true harmony, and in this tune
turn families, passions, histories, planets, all.

The Syntax of Seasons

Autumn was adjectival. I recall
a gray, dank, gnarled spell
when all wore fall-quality, a bare
mutating atmosphere.

Winter hardened into nouns. Withdrawn
in lamplight, I would crown
the cold with thought-exactitude, would claim
the drear air with a name.

In spring, all language loosened and became
less in demand, limping, lame,
before the bursting days. What told
was tongue-tied wonder at the green and gold.

Steeped now in summer, though our chattering
rises and falls, occasional as birdsong,
we fall to silence under the burning sun,
and feel the great verbs run.

Flying Time

The man in the seat in front
is bald. As he reclines
his shining pate toward me,
I look up from the map
on my knee and read into his head
the red veins that connect
St Louis with Chicago,
Phoenix with Washington.
A coastline of gray hair surrounds
his neat, skintight America,
luminous, like a mirror.
I cannot see his face
but might catch sight of my own,
might face my alien
and anxious eyes. Does he
hold an America in his head,
and is the man behind
reading the back of my head?
My hair obscures my mind.
The seat-belt sign is on.
The sky is letting us down.
What waits on the ground?
Some solid, sure America,
prepared to take us in
from the nowhere of the air,
bald, mad, lost as we are?

The Day The Weather Broke

Last out in the raining weather, a girl and I.
drip in the hazy light while cars slur by,
    and the single drizzling reason
    of rain in an alien season
turns us *to* each other till a train arrives,
to share, by bond of wetness, our wet lives.

Although, for talk, we can find to put our thumb on
    only the rain in common,
is this what love is – that we draw together
    in the inhuman weather,
strangers, who pool our sheltered selves and take,
    for the sky's sake,
this luck, to be caught without our usual cloak
    the day the weather broke?

Growing, Flying, Happening

Say the soft bird's name, but do not be surprised
to see it fall
headlong, struck skyless, into its pigeonhole –
columba palumbus and you have it dead,
wedged, neat, unwinged in your head.

That that black-backed tatter-winged thing
straking the harbour water and then plummeting
down, to come up, sleek head a-cock,
a minted herring shining in its beak,
is a *guillemot*, is neither here nor there
in the amazement of its rising,
wings slicing the stiff salt air.

That of that spindling spear-leaved plant,
wearing the palest purple umbel,
many-headed, blue-tinted, stilt-stalked
at the stream-edge, one should say briefly
angelica, is by-the-way (though grant
the name itself to be beautiful).
Grant too that any name
makes its own music, that *bryony, sally-my-handsome*
burst at their sound into flower,
and that *falcon* and *phalarope* fly off in the ear,
still,
names are for saying at home.

The point is seeing – the grace
beyond recognition, the ways
of the bird rising, unnamed, unknown,
beyond the range of language, beyond its noun.
Eyes open on growing, flying, happening,
and go on opening. Manifold, the world
dawns on unrecognising, realising eyes.
Amazement is the thing.
Not love, but the astonishment of loving.

Living in Time

This morning, overpowered
by weather and discontent,
I climb the escarpment
and manage to be lost
in watching for an hour

the pointlessness of swallows
which have nothing to do with me
larruping through the trees,
and in curling thrown stones
into the dull valley.

Yet on my slow way home,
the dark selves from the study
fall into step beside me
and one by one resume
the morning's lame conundrum.

Bird-minded now, I answer
loosely, light-heartedly,
but their presences tower.
Looking becomes a question.
Thought glooms the day.

Then, unexpectedly,
she is waiting in the doorway,
ready with something to say,
so much herself, so beautifully
occupying her body

that I am all wonder,
beyond mind and words.
She wears the day about her.
The dark ones disappear, and birds
reclaim the particular air.

Better to live in time.
The moment is her home.
Better to leave it
as something that is, that happens
as luck will have it.

Curiosity

may have killed the cat. More likely,
the cat was just unlucky, or else curious
to see what death was like, having no cause
to go on licking paws, or fathering
litter on litter of kittens, predictably.

Nevertheless, to be curious
is dangerous enough. To distrust
what is always said, what seems,
to ask odd questions, interfere in dreams,
smell rats, leave home, have hunches,
does not endear cats to those doggy circles
where well-smelt baskets, suitable wives, good lunches
are the order of things, and where prevails
much wagging of incurious heads and tails.

Face it. Curiosity
will not cause us to die –
only lack of it will.
Never to want to see
the other side of the hill
or that improbable country
where living is an idyll
(although a probable hell)
would kill us all.
Only the curious
have if they live a tale
worth telling at all.

Dogs say cats love too much, are irresponsible,
are dangerous, marry too many wives,
desert their children, chill all dinner tables
with tales of their nine lives.

Well, they are lucky. Let them be
nine-lived and contradictory,
curious enough to change, prepared to pay
the cat-price, which is to die
and die again and again,
each time with no less pain.
A cat-minority of one
is all that can be counted on
to tell the truth; and what cats have to tell
on each return from hell
is this: that dying is what the living do,
that dying is what the loving do,
and that dead dogs are those who never know
that dying is what, to live, each has to do.

Disguises

My selves, my presences,
like uniforms and suits,
some stiff, some soiled, some threadbare,
and not all easy-fitting,
hang somewhere in the house.

A friend or a misfortune
will force me, on occasion,
into a sober habit,
uncomfortably formal,
in keeping, though unwise.

But otherwise I wear
something old and easy,
with little thought to please,
nor a glance in the mirror,
nor a care for size;

being caught, in consequence,
sporting the wrong color
in inappropriate weather –
odd shirts, uneven socks,
and most unsuitable ties.

I should have a tailor,
or, failing him, a mirror;
but being possessed of neither,
I sit in my stubborn skin and count
all clothing as disguise.

Propinquity

is the province of cats. Living by accident,
lapping the food at hand or sleeking down
in an adjacent lap when sleep occurs to them,
never aspiring to consistency
in homes or partners, unaware of property,
cats take their chances, love by need or nearness
as long as the need lasts, as long as the nearness
is near enough. The code of cats is simply
to take what comes. And those poor souls who claim
to own a cat, who long to recognise
in bland and narrowing eyes a look like love,
are bound to suffer should they expect
cats to come purring punctually home.
Home is only where the food and the fire are,
but might be anywhere. Cats fall on their feet,
nurse their own wounds, attend to their own laundry,
and purr at appropriate times. O folly, folly,
to love a cat, and yet
we dress with love the distance that they keep,
the hair-raising way they have, and easily blame

all their abandoned litters and torn ears
on some marauding tiger, well aware
that cats themselves do not care.

Yet part of us is cat. Confess –
love turns on accident and needs
nearness; and the various selves we have
accrue from our cat-wanderings, our chance
crossings. Imagination prowls at night,
cat-like, among odd possibilities.
Only our dog-sense brings us faithfully home,
makes meaning out of accident, keeps faith,
and, cat-and-dog, the arguments go at it.
But every night, outside, cat-voices call
us out to take a chance, to leave
the safety of our baskets and to let
what happens happen. 'Live, live!' they catcall.
'Each moment is your next! Propinquity,
propinquity is all!'

Ghosts

Never to see ghosts? Then to be
haunted by what is, only, to believe that glass
is for looking through, that rooms too can be empty,
the past past, deeds done,
that sleep, however troubled, is your own.
Do the dead lie down, then? Are blind men blind?
Does love rest in the senses? Do lights go out?
And what is that shifting, shifting in the mind?
The wind?

No, they are with us. Let your ear be gentle.
At dawn or owl-cry, over doorway and lintel,

theirs are the voices moving night towards morning,
the garden's grief, the river's warning.
Their curious presence in a kiss,
the past quivering in what is,
our words odd-sounding, not our own –
how can we think we sleep alone?

What do they have to tell? If we can hear them,
their voices are denials of all dying,
faint, like a lost bell-tone, lying
beyond sound or belief, in the oblique
reach of the sense through layers of recognition … .
Ghost by my desk, speak, speak.

Pigeons

On the crooked arm of Columbus, on his cloak,
they mimic his blind and statuary stare,
and the chipped profiles of his handmaidens
they adorn with droppings. Over the loud square,
from all the arms and ledges of their rest,
only a breadcrust or a bell unshelves them.
Adding to Atlas' globe, they dispose themselves
with a fat propriety, and pose as garlands
importantly about his burdened shoulders.
Occasionally a lift of wind uncarves them.

Stone becomes them; they in their turn become it.
Their opal eyes have a monumental cast.
And, in a maze of noise,
their quiet *croomb croomb* dignifies the spaces,
suggesting the sound of silence. On cobbled islands,
marooned in tantrums of traffic, they know their place.
Faithful and anonymous, like servants,
they never beg, but properly receive.

Arriving in rainbows of oil-and-water feathers,
they fountain down from buttresses and outcrops,
from Fontainebleau and London,
and, perched on the margins of roofs, with a gargoyle look,
they note, from an edge of air, with hooded eyes,
the city slowly lessening the sky.

All praise to them who nightly in the parks
keep peace for us; who, cosmopolitan,
patrol and people all cathedralled places,
the paved courts of the past, pompous as keepers,
and easily, lazily haunt and inhabit
St Paul's, St Peter's, or the Madeleine –
a sober race of messengers and custodians,
neat in their international uniforms,
alighting with a word perhaps from Rome.
Permanence is their business, space and time
their special preservations; and wherever
the great stone men we save from death are stationed,
appropriately on the head of each is perched,
as though for ever, his appointed pigeon.

Cat-Faith

As a cat, caught by the door opening,
on the perilous top shelf, red-jawed and raspberry-clawed,
lets itself fall floorward without looking,
sure by cat-instinct it will find the ground,
where innocence is; and falls
anyhow, in a furball, so fast that the eye
misses the twist and trust
that come from having fallen before,
and only notices cat silking away,
crime inconceivable in so meek a walk:

so do we let ourselves fall morningward
through shelves of dream. When, libertine at dark,
we let the visions in, and the black window
grotesques us back, our world unbalances.
Many-faced monsters of our own devising
jostle on the verge of sleep, as the room
loses its edges and grows hazed and haunted
by words murmured or by woes remembered,
till, sleep-dissolved, we fall, the known world leaves us,
and room and dream and self and safety melt
into a final madness, where any landscape
may easily curdle, and the dead cry out ...

but ultimately, it ebbs. Voices recede.
The pale square of the window glows and stays.
Slowly the room arrives and dawns, and we
arrive in our selves. Last night, last week, the past
leak back, awake. As light solidifies,
dream dims. Outside, the washed hush of the garden
waits patiently and, newcomers from death,
how gratefully we draw its breath!
Yet, to endure that unknown night by night,
must we not be sure, with cat-insight,
we can afford its terrors, and that full day
will find us at the desk, sane, unafraid –
cheeks shaven, letters written, bills paid?

Foreigners

Owls, like monks of a rare, feathered order,
haunt one aloof, lopped tower in this
unlikely city, cresting the broken stones
like ghosts at dusk, watchful, wary,
describing soft, slow curves in the falling sky.

Supremely odd and patiently oblivious
to all but wind and owlhood, they tatter
the evening air with their broad, sooty wings.
And over all, the tower seems content
with its alien colony. For whose is a city?

Yet below, the jabbering birds of the sprawled suburbs
complain from the lower roofs, look up from crusts
and blame owls for the dust, for all the dismal
workaday winging. The atmosphere is crowded,
to their native eyes, with a woeful weight of owls.

What do the owls answer? To wit, nothing.
And sure enough, with time passing, the tower
becomes a landmark mentioned in the guidebooks
with owls as appropriate appendages. The city
absorbs them into its anonymous air.

Now other birds alight on the battlements,
occasionally singing. Not worthwhile to war
over a lack of crumbs, in alien weather.
Who gives a hoot, say owls. The wind is common.
Let all poor birds be brothers under the feather.

Outlook, Uncertain

No season
brings conclusion.

Each year,
through heartache, nightmare,

true loves alter,
marriages falter,

and lovers illumine
the antique design,

apart, together,
foolish as weather,

right as rain,
sure as ruin.

Must you, then, and I
adjust the whole sky

over every morning?
Or else, submitting

to cloud and storm,
enact the same

lugubrious ending,
new lives pending?

Stalemate

Shrill interruption
of children's voices
raised in the garden.
Two of them stand
face to face,
each in one hand
weighing a stone,
each on his own
rigid ground.

You drop your stone,
then I'll drop mine.
No, you first.
Put yours down.
But if I do,
you'll throw yours.
Promise I won't.
I don't believe you.
Cross your heart?
Cross my heart.

Easy to call
the children in
before blows fall,
but not to settle
the ruffled feel
the garden has
as they both echo
the endless bicker
of lovers and statesmen,
learnt so soon.

Who began it?
Now, no matter.

The air is taut
with accusation.
Despair falls
like a cold stone
crossing the heart.
How did it start?
A children's quarrel.
What is its end?
The death of love.
The doom of all.

What's What

Most people know
the story of how
the frog was a prince
and the dragon was ticklish,
or how the princess
grew fat in the end;
nevertheless,
think of the chance
the youngest son took –
gloom to the left of him,
groans to the right of him,
no spell to tell him
which way to take,
no map, no book,
no real interest.
All he could say was
'Maybe I'm me'
but he knew not to trust
the wizards who seemed,
the bird with the breast

of too many colours,
the princess who hummed
too perfect a song.
The going was not good
but his curious head
said over and over
ridiculous words
like *quince* and *fray bentos*
all through the wood.
'Yes,' he said firmly,
'nobody pays me,
nobody knows me,
so I will decide
which tree will amaze me
when I see a leaf
I can be sure of.
Whom do I listen to?
Not that toad
with the gem in its head,
nor that mole that mumbles
precise directions,
nor the nice wizard,
so soft and helpful,
nor mild old women
gathering wood.
It's that clumsy bird
who looks askance
with only one eye –
untidy feathers,
flying absent-mindedly,
out in all weathers,
little to say –
he's for me.
He's not after
a cut of the treasure.
He knows well
that he's going nowhere

and, what's more,
he doesn't care.

If I'd listened to witches
and looked in crystals,
I'd be expert
at going wrong,
but I know my birdsong.
Hearing his *tip-tippy*,
I know who *he* is.
I'll go *his* way.

Needless to say,
the youngest son won
with enough to go on;
and the one-eyed bird,
whoever he was,
went *tip-tip-tippy*
to pleasure his own
well-worn feathers,
over and over,
with no one to hear . . .

Then, one day,
the youngest son
had a youngest son,
and so on.

In Memory of My Uncle Timothy

His name, they told me afterwards, was Able,
and he came, in yellow boots and a hat, and stood by the table
beside my Uncle Timmy, who went mad
later, and was a trouble to my Dad.
Uncle Tim said shakily 'God, it's not you!'
but whoever he was, it was. So Tim took off his shoe,
shook it, and held it upside down. Out fell
a photograph of Grace, a sprig of fennel,
a bent crown piece, and a small gold key as well.
Tim spilt them in this man's lap, and he
 – you'll not believe it – took out his eye
(glass, it was), and turned it over. On the back
was a crooked keyhole and a lock.
So he took Tim's key (he did, he did!)
and put it in. Up sprung a kind of lid.
He shoved it under Tim's nose. 'Holy God!'
cried Tim. I looked, in the nick, before it closed.

Inside, upside down, was a tiny man
in a hat like Able's, with yellow boots on,
the spitting image of this living Able,
and there were Tim and me, upside down at the table,
and in the man's hand . . . but he quickly locked his eye,
tucking carefully away the key,
and put the thing crookedly back in his face,
gave Uncle the coin and the photograph of Grace,
stuck the sprig of fennel in his hat,
and off he went. 'Uncle Tim' I cried, 'what was that?'
I remember his face, but now I forget what he said.
Anyway, now Tim's dead.

Calenture

He never lives to tell,
but other men bring back the tale

of how, after days of gazing at the sea
unfolding itself incessantly and greenly –
hillsides of water crested with clouds of foam –
he, heavy with a fading dream of home,
clambers aloft one morning and, looking down,
cries out at seeing a different green –
farms, woods, grasslands, an extending plain,
hazy meadows, a long tree-fledged horizon,
his ship riding deep in rippled grain,
swallows flashing in the halcyon sun,
the road well-known to him, the house, the garden,
figures at the gate – and, foundering in his passion,
he suddenly climbs down and begins to run.
Dazed by his joy, the others watch him drown.

Such calenture, they say,
is not unknown in lovers long at sea
yet such a like fever did she make in me
this green-leaved summer morning, that I,
seeing her confirm a wish made lovingly,
felt gate, trees, grass, birds, garden glimmer over,
a ripple cross her face, the sky quiver,
the cropped lawn away in waves, the house founder
the light break into flecks, the path shimmer
till, finding her eyes clear and true at the centre,
I walked toward her on the flowering water.

Me to You

I

Summer's gone brown and, with it,
our wanderings in the shires, our ways.
Look at us now.
A shuttered house drips in Moroccan rain.
A mill sits ghostly in the green of France.

Beaches are empty now of all but pebbles.
But still, at crossroads, in senorial gardens,
we meet, sleep, wrangle, part, meet, part,
making a lodging of the heart.

Now that the sea begins to dull with winter,
and I so far, and you so far
(and home further than either),
write me a long letter,
as if from home.
Tell me about the snowfalls
at night, and tell me how we'd sit in firelight,
hearing dogs huff in sleep, hearing the geese
hiss in the barn, hearing the horse clop home.
Say how the waterfall sounds, and how the weeds
trail in the slithering river.
Write me about the weather.

Perhaps
a letter across water,
something like this, but better,
would almost move us strangely
closer to home.

Write, and I'll come.

II

All day I have been writing you a letter.

Now, after hours of gazing at the page
and watching the screen of rain, I have enacted
a flow of endless letters in my head
(all of them different) and not one
in any written shape to send.
Those letters never end.

In between pages of wishing, I walked to the river
and wrote you of how the water
wrinkles and eddies and wanders away.
That was easier to say.

I wrote of how the snow
had fallen and turned blue,
and how the bush you wanted
could not be planted.

Some pages were all remembering – the places,
faces, frontiers, rooms, and days we went through
ages ago.
(Do you do this too?)
Always coming back to snow.

Mostly an endless, useless run of questions.
How are you now? How is it there?
Who will you and I
be in a year?
Who are we now?

Oh no,
there is no letter to send you, only this stream
of disconnected brooding, this rhythm
of wanting, cumbersome
in words, lame.

Come.

A Lesson for Beautiful Women

Gazing and gazing in the glass,
she might have noticed slow cotillions pass
and might have seen
a blur of others in the antique green.
Transfixed instead,
she learned the inclinations of her neat small head
and, startling her own surprise,
wondered at the wonder in her jewelled eyes.

Gardens of rainbow and russet might have caught her
but, leaning over goldfish water,
she watched the red carp emphasise her mouth,
saw underneath
the long green weeds lace in
through a transparency of face and skin,
smiled at herself smiling reflectively,
lending a new complexion to the sky.

In service to her beauty
long mornings lengthened to a duty
patiently served before the triple mirror
whose six eyes sent her many a time in terror
to hide in rows of whispering dresses;
but her glass soul her own three goddesses
pursued, and if she turned away,
the same three mouths would breathe 'Obey, obey!'

And in procession, young men princely came,
ambassadors to her cool perfect kingdom.
Set at a distance by their praise,
she watched their unspeaking eyes adore her face.
Inside, her still self waited. Nothing moved.
Finally, by three husbands richly loved
(none of them young), she drifted into death,
the glass clouding with her last moist breath.

Changed into legend, she was given rest;
and, left alone at last,
the small mim servant shuttered in her being
peeped mousily out; and seeing
the imperious mirrors glazed and still,
whimpered forlornly down the dark hall
'Oh, grieve for my body, who would not let me be.
She, not I, was a most beautiful lady.'

In Such a Poise is Love

Why should a hint of winter
shadow the window while the insects enter,
or a feel of snowfall, taking corners off
the rough wall and the roof,
while the sun, hanging in the sky,
hotly denies its contrary?

As if it knew all future must entail
probable tempered by improbable,
so the mind wanders to the unforeseen,
and the eye, waking, poises between
shock and recognition – the clothes, the chair,
bewildering, familiar.

In such a poise is love. But who
can keep the balance true,
can stay in the day's surprise, moving
between twin fears, of losing and of having?
Who has not, in love's fever,
insisted on the fatal vow, 'for ever,'
and sensed, before the words are gone,
the doom in them dawn?

For Ring-Givers

Given the gift of a ring,
what circle does it close?
What does it say, passing
from lover to lover?
That love, encircled so,
rings for ever?

Or is it the round of love?
Does the ring say
'So must love move,
and in its altering weather,
you two will turn away
as now you turn together'?

Is the ring given or lent?
Does love ring round us
or do we ring round it?
Ring-giver, be warned.
Are you, in turn, expecting
love or the ring returned?

Quarrels

I can feel a quarrel blowing up in your body,
as old salts can smell storms
which are still fretting under the horizon,
before your eyes have flashed their first alarms.

Whatever the reason, the reason is not the reason,
It's a weather. It's a wellhead about to blaze gas,
flaring up when you suddenly stumble over
an alien presence in your private space.

You face me, eyes slitted like a cat's.
I can feel your nails uncurling.
The tendons in your neck twang with anger.
Your face is liquid as it is in loving.

Marking how often you say 'always' and 'never',
I on my side grow icy, tall, and thin
until, with watching you, I forget to listen,
and am burned through and through with your high passion.

Face to face, like wrestlers or lovers,
we spit it out. Your words nip, like bites.
Your argument's a small, tenacious creature
I try to stomp on with great logical boots.

Dear angry one, let the boots and the skittering beast
chase wildly round the room like Tom and Jerry
or who and why. Let us withdraw and watch them,
but side by side, not nose to nose and wary.

That is the only way we'll disentangle
the quarrel from ourselves and switch it off.
Not face to face. The sparks of confrontation
too easily ignite a rage like love.

The he–with–her subsides, the I–with–you
looms into place. So we fold up the words
and, with a movement much like waking up,
we turn the weather down, and turn towards.

A Leavetaking

What a day we parted on!
Sludge. Not a wink of sun.
Heavy headlines, traffic breakdowns.
Three damp children dressed as clowns.
A sobbing drunk on the corner, reeling.
The sky as smoke-stained as a ceiling.
Any two but she and I
would have been glad to say good-bye.
The houses bowed their heads in rows
as, with rain running down my nose,
I watched her go her ways,
a bright true tear across a dirty face.

Small Sad Song

I am a lady
three feet small.
My voice is thin
but listen, listen.
Before I die
my modest death,
tell me what gentlemen
do with great ladies,
for thigh-high now
are the thoughts I think.

Once as a girl
I knew how to smile.
My world stayed small
as my playmates mountained.

My mother mocked me.
Dogs plagued me.
Now I am doomed
to dwell among elephants.
Sometimes I fall
in love with a bird.

I move amongst
donkeys and monkeys.
Dwarfs paw me
with stubby hands.
I cannot look at them.
There are no friends
of a suitable size.
Giants tease me.
Men do not choose me.
A hunchback loves me.

If someone moved me,
I might make
monstrous poems,
vast as my dreams;
but what can come
from a thumbnail lady?
Words like watch-ticks,
whispers, twitterings,
suitable tinkles,
nothing at all.

The Figures on the Frieze

Darkness wears off and, dawning into light,
they find themselves unmagically together.
He sees the stains of morning in her face.
She shivers, distant in his bitter weather.

Diminishing of legend sets him brooding.
Great goddess-figures conjured from his book
blur what he sees with bafflement of wishing.
Sulky, she feels his fierce, accusing look.

Familiar as her own, his body's landscape
seems harsh and dull to her habitual eyes.
Mystery leaves, and, mercilessly flying,
the blind fiends come, emboldened by her cries.

Avoiding simple reach of hand for hand
(which would surrender pride) by noon they stand
withdrawn from touch, reproachfully alone,
small in each other's eyes, tall in their own.

Wild with their misery, they entangle now
in baffling agonies of why and how.
Afternoon glimmers, and they wound anew,
flesh, nerve, bone, gristle in each other's view.

'What have you done to me?' From each proud heart,
new phantoms walk in the deceiving air.
As the light fails, each is consumed apart,
he by his ogre vision, she by her fire.

When night falls, out of a despair of daylight,
they strike the lying attitudes of love,
and through the perturbations of their bodies,
each feels the amazing, murderous legends move.

For Her Sake

Her world is all aware. She reads
omens in small happenings, the fall of a teaspoon,
flurries of birds, a cat's back arching,
words unspoken, wine spilt.
She will notice moods in handwriting,
be tuned to feelings in a room,
sense ill luck in a house, take heed of ghosts,
hear children cry before the sound has reached her,
stay unperturbed in storms, keep silence
where speech would spoil. Days are her changes,
weather her time.

Whether it be becalmed in cool mornings
of air and water, or thunderstruck through nights
where flesh craves and is answered, in her, love
knows no division, is an incarnation
of all her wonder, as she makes
madness subside, and all thought-splintered things
grow whole again.

Look below. She walks in the garden,
preoccupied with paths, head bent,
beautiful, not at rest, as objects are,
but moving, in the fleck of light and shade.
Her ways are hers, not mine. Pointless to make
my sense of her, or claim her faithfulness.
She is as women are, aware
of her own mystery, in her way faithful
to flowers and days; and from the window's distance
I watch her, haunted by her otherness.

Well to love true women, whose whims are wise,
whose world is warm, whose home is time,
and well to pleasure them, since, last of all,

they are the truth which men must tell,
and in their pleasure, houses lighten,
gardens grow fruitful, and true tales are told.
Well to move from mind's distance
into their aura, where the air
is shifting, intimate, particular.

And of true women, she, whose eyes illumine
this day I wake in – well to mark
her weather, how her look is candid,
her voice clear-toned, her heart private,
her love both wild and reticent.
Well to praise and please her, well to make
this for her sake.

Where Truth Lies

Maps, once made,
leave the impression of a place gone dead.

Words, once said,
anchor the swirlings in the head.

Vows, once taken,
waste in the shadows of a time forsaken.

Oh, understand
how the mind's landscape grows from shifting sand,

how where we are
is half on solid ground, half head-in-air,

a twilit zone
where changing flesh and changeless ghost are one,

and what is true
lies between you and the idea of you –

a friction,
restless, between the fact and the fiction.

A Lesson in Music

Play the tune again: but this time
with more regard for the movement at the source of it
and less attention to time. Time falls
curiously in the course of it.

Play the tune again: not watching
your fingering, but forgetting, letting flow
the sound till it surrounds you. Do not count
or even think. Let go.

Play the tune again: but try to be
nobody, nothing, as though the pace
of the sound were your heart beating, as though
the music were your face.

Play the tune again. It should be easier
to think less every time of the notes, of the measure.
It is all an arrangement of silence. Be silent, and then
play it for your pleasure.

Play the tune again; and this time, when it ends,
do not ask me what I think. Feel what is happening
strangely in the room as the sound glooms over
you, me, everything.

Now,
play the tune again.

A Lesson in Handwriting

Try first this figure 2,
how, from the point of the pen,
clockwise it unwinds itself
downward to the line,
making itself a pedestal to stand on.
Watch now. Before your eyes it becomes a swan
drifting across the page, its neck so carefully
poised, its inky eye
lowered in modesty.
As you continue, soon,
between the thin blue lines,
swan after swan sails beautifully past you,
margin to margin, 2 by 2 by 2,
a handwritten swirl of swans.
Under them now unroll
the soft, curled pillows of the 6's,
the acrobatic 3's, the angular 7's,
the hourglass 8's and the neat tadpole 9's,
each passing in review
on stilts and wheels and platforms
in copybook order.

Turn the page, for now
comes the alphabet, an eccentric
parade of odd characters. Initially you may tangle
now and again in a loop or a twirl,
but patience, patience. Each in time will dawn
as faces and animals do, familiar,
laughable, crooked, quirky.
Begin with the letter S. Already
it twists away from the point like a snake or a watchspring,
coiled up and back to strike. SSSS, it says,
hissing and slithering off into the ferns of the F's.

Next comes a line of stately Q's floating
just off the ground, tethered by their tails,
over the folded arms of the W's
and the akimbo M's. Open-eyed, the O's
roll after them like bubbles or balloons
flown by the serious three-tongued E's.
See now how the page fills up
with all the furniture of writing – the armchair H's,
the ladders and trestles of A's and Y's and X's,
the T-shaped tables and the upholstered B's.
The pen abandons a whole scaffolding
of struts and braces, springs and balances,
on which will rest eventually
the weight of a written world, storey on storey
of words and signatures, all the long-drawn-out telling
that pens become repositories of.
These are now your care, and you may give them
whatever slant or human twist you wish,
if it should please you. But you will not alter
their scrawled authority, durable
as stone, silent, grave, oblivious
of all you make them tell.

Tomorrow, words begin.

The Academy

I do not think of the academy
in the whirl of days. It does not change. I do.
The place hangs in my past like an engraving.
I went back once to lay a wreath on it,
and met discarded selves I scarcely knew.

It has a lingering aura, leather bindings,
a smell of varnish and formaldehyde,

a certain dusty holiness in the cloisters.
We used to race our horses on the sand
away from it, manes flying, breathing hard.

Trailing to the library of an afternoon,
we saw the ivy crawling underneath
the labyrinthine bars on the window ledges.
I remember the thin librarian's look of hate
as we left book holes in her shelves, like missing teeth.

On evenings doomed by bells, we felt the sea
creep up, we heard the temperamental gulls
wheeling in clouds about the kneeworn chapel.
They keened on the knifing wind like student souls.
Yet we would dent the stones with our own footfalls.

Students still populate the place, bright starlings,
their notebooks filled with scribbled parrot-answers
to questions they unravel every evening
in lamplit pools of spreading argument.
They slash the air with theory, like fencers.

Where is the small, damp-browed professor now?
Students have pushed him out to sea in a boat
of lecture-notes. Look, he bursts into flame!
How glorious a going for one whose words
had never struck a spark on the whale-road.

And you will find retainers at their posts,
wearing their suits of age, brass buttons, flannel,
patrolling lawns they crop with careful scissors.
They still will be in silver-haired attendance
to draw lines through our entries in the annals.

It is illusion, the academy.
In truth, the ideal talking-place to die.
Only the landscape keeps a sense of growing.
The towers are floating on a shifting sea.
You did not tell the truth there, nor did I.

Think of the process – moments becoming poems
which stiffen into books in the library,
and later, lectures, books about the books,
footnotes and dates, a stone obituary.
Do you wonder that I shun the academy?

It anticipates my dying, turns to stone
too quickly for my taste. It is a language
nobody speaks, refined to ritual:
the precise writing on the blackboard wall,
the drone of requiem in the lecture hall.

I do not think much of the academy
in the drift of days. It does not change. I do.
This poem will occupy the library
but I will not. I have not done with doing.
I did not know the truth there, nor did you.

The O-Filler

One noon in the library, I watched a man –
imagine! – filling in O's, a little, rumpled
nobody of a man, who licked his stub of pencil
and leaned over every O with a loving care,
shading it neatly, exactly to its edges
until the open pages
were pocked and dotted with solid O's, like towns
and capitals on a map. And yet, so peppered,
the book appeared inhabited and complete.

That whole afternoon, as the light outside softened
and the library groaned woodenly,
he worked and worked, his o-so-patient shading
descending like an eyelid over each open O
for page after page. Not once did he miss one,

or hover even a moment over an *a*
or an *e* or a *p* or a *g*. Only the O's –
oodles of O's, O's multitudinous, O's manifold,
O's italic and roman.
And what light on his crumpled face when he discovered –
as I supposed – odd words like *zoo* and *ooze*,
polo, *oolong* and *odontology*!

Think now. In that limitless library,
all round the steep-shelved walls, bulging in their bindings,
books stood, waiting. Heaven knows how many
he had so far filled, but still there remained
uncountable volumes of O-laden prose, and odes
with inflated capital O's (in the manner of Shelley),
O-bearing Bibles and biographies,
even whole sections devoted to O alone,
all his for the filling. Glory, glory, glory!
How utterly open and endless the world must have
                                seemed to him,
how round and ample! Think of it. A pencil
was all he needed. Life was one wide O.

And why, at the end of things, should O's not be closed
as eyes are? I envied him, for in my place
across the table from him, had I accomplished
anything as firm as he had, or as fruitful?
What could I show? A handful of scrawled lines,
an afternoon yawned and wondered away,
and a growing realisation that in time
even my scribbled words would come
under his grubby thumb, and the blinds be drawn
on all my O's, with only this thought for comfort –
that when he comes to this poem, a proper joy
may amaze his wizened face and, o, a pure pleasure
make his relentless pencil quiver.

The Fall

He teeters along the crumbling top
of the garden wall and calls, 'Look up,
Papa, look up! I'm flying . . .' till,
in a sudden foreseen spasm, I see him fall.

Terrible
when fear cries to the senses, when the whirl
of the possible drowns the real. Falling
is a fright in me. I call
and move in time to catch
his small, sweat-beaded body,
still thrilled with the air.
'I flew, Papa, I flew!'
'I know, child, I know.'

Daedalus

My son has birds in his head.

I know them now. I catch
the pitch of their calls, their shrill
cacophonies, their chitterings, their coos.
They hover behind his eyes and come to rest
on a branch, on a book, grow still,
claws curled, wings furled.
His is a bird world.

I learn the flutter of his moods,
his moments of swoop and soar.
From the ground I feel him try
the limits of the air –

sudden lift, sudden terror –
and move in time to cradle
his quivering, feathered fear.

At evening, in the tower,
I see him to sleep and see
the hooding-over of eyes,
the slow folding of wings.
I wake to his morning twitterings,
to the *croomb* of his becoming.

He chooses his selves – wren, hawk,
swallow or owl – to explore
the trees and rooftops of his heady wishing.
Tomtit, birdie.
Am I to call him down, to give him
a grounding, teach him gravity?
Gently, gently.
Time tells us what we weigh, and soon enough
his feet will reach the ground.
Age, like a cage, will enclose him.
So the wise men said.

My son has birds in his head.

The Spiral

The seasons of this year are in my luggage.
Now, lifting the last picture from the wall,
I close the eyes of the room. Each footfall
clatters on the bareness of the stair.
The family ghosts fade in the hanging air.
Mirrors reflect the silence. There is no message.
I wait in the still hall for a car to come.
Behind, the house will dwindle to a name.

Places, addresses, faces left behind.
The present is a devious wind
obliterating days and promises.
Tomorrow is a tinker's guess.
Marooned in cities, dreaming of greenness,
or dazed by journeys, dreading to arrive –
change, change is where I live.

For possibility,
I choose to leave behind
each language, each country.
Will this place be an end,
or will there be one other,
truer, rarer?

Often now, in dream,
abandoned landscapes come,
figuring a constant theme:
Have you left us behind?
What have you still to find?

Across the spiral distance,
through time and turbulence,
the rooted self in me
maps out its true country.

And, as my father found
his own small weathered island,
so will I come to ground

where that small man, my son,
can put his years on.

For him, too, time will turn.

Whithorn Manse

I knew it as Eden,
that lost walled garden,
past the green edge
of priory and village;
and, beyond it, the house,
withdrawn, white,
one window alight.

Returning, I wonder,
idly, uneasily,
what eyes from inside
look out now, not in,
as once mine did,
and what might grant me
a right of entry?

Is it never dead, then,
that need of an Eden?

Even this evening,
estranged by age,
I ogle that light
with a child's greed,
wistfully claiming
lost prerogatives
of homecoming.

Weathering

I am old enough now for a tree
once planted, knee high, to have grown to be
twenty times me,

and to have seen babies marry, and heroes grow deaf –
but that's enough meaning-of-life.
It's living through time we ought to be connoisseurs of.

From wearing a face all this time, I am made aware
of the maps faces are, of the inside wear and tear.
I take to faces that have come far.

In my father's carved face, the bright eye
he sometimes would look out of, seeing a long way
through all the tree-rings of his history.

I am awed by how things weather: an oak mantel
in the house in Spain, fingered to a sheen,
the marks of hands leaned into the lintel,

the tokens in the drawer I sometimes touch –
a crystal lived-in on a trip, the watch
my father's wrist wore to a thin gold sandwich.

It is an equilibrium
which breasts the cresting seasons but still stays calm
and keeps warm. It deserves a good name.

Weathering. Patina, gloss, and whorl.
The trunk of the almond tree, gnarled but still fruitful.
Weathering is what I would like to do well.

Mandala Dilemma

Counters

ounce

dice

trice

quartz

quince

sago

serpent

oxygen

nitrogen

denim

instant

distant

tryst

catalyst

quest

sycamore

sophomore

oculist

novelist

dentist

acreage

brokerage

cribbage

carthage

cage

sink

sentiment

ointment

nutmeg

doom

archery

butchery

treachery

taproom

tomb

sermon

cinnamon

apron

nunnery

density

I only went out for a walk, and finally concluded to stay out till sundown, for going out, I found, was really going in.

John Muir

WRITERS

Ask for Nicolás Catari

Somehow (and it would be worth someone's patient attention to work out just why), Latin America remains curiously fictive in the Western mind – in the minds, at least, of those who have never been driven, out of curiosity or circumstance, to find out about it. Perhaps 'filmic' would be a better word than 'fictive' – the image of Latin America in the popular consciousness seems to stem from a mixture of Carmen Miranda, Cantinflas, and the cha-cha-cha, with a script that veers from Woody Allen banana republic to Monte-zuma-sized epic. For the British, the continent has an aura of remote geography lessons, which is where I first met it – always the least pawed page in the atlas. It was only when I lived in Spain that Latin America began to take on substance, as the New World. Traditionally, older Spaniards have much the same attitude toward the Latin American countries as the more unbending English toward the United States ('Tell me, is it true that in the United States one lunches at the chemist's?'), but in Spain I talked with real Latin Americans – or real Peruvians and Chileans and Colombians, rather, for Latin America is something of a geographical myth – and eventually, in a series of journeys there, I learned the extent of my ignorance, and have been chipping away at it ever since. In the course of conversations about Latin America, however, I still find myself having to draw maps in the air. The geography of the continent gets in the way of its humanity: people know infinitely less about the character of Venezuelans and Bolivians than they do about Serbs and Croats or the peoples of the Middle East. And if one uses the term 'Latin America' correctly – to embrace the Spanish-, Portuguese-, and French-speaking countries of the South American continent, Central America, and the Caribbean – the physical, political, and cultural complexity of such a mess of

99

national entities looks too forbidding to disentangle, and the continent is left in shadow, on the fringes of serious attention.

One solid piece of reassurance comes to me annually, in the form of *The South American Handbook,* a publication that goes a long way to bringing Latin America into the light. It has had a singular evolution: it began in 1921 as a fairly sketchy guide for British businessmen going 'out' to that continent, and, apart from a few wartime gaps, it has appeared every December since, in an ever-fattening form; the 1977 edition is the fifty-third. The *Handbook* was originally put together by the Federation of British Industries and later backed by British shipping interests, which were then powerfully connected to Latin America. Six years ago, when these business interests withdrew their support and it looked as if publication might cease, the *Handbook* was taken over by the printing firm that produced it, Dawson & Goodall, in Bath, in the West of England – as well-groomed and un-Latin-American a place as there is. Its thousand-odd pages of small and busy print clamor for the attention of anyone who is keen on armchair travel or is thirsty for sheer information.

Curiously, *The South American Handbook* remains almost unknown except to a small and passionate band of initiates who have traveled in Latin America in its company, and who, as a result, stay loyal to it forever, and can usually recite chosen passages by heart. In the 1950s, the *Handbook* began asking its readers to correct its information from the field, and now it draws on a flood of correspondence for factual information and a whimsically varying prose manner. With such meticulous help from its correspondents, the *Handbook* updates itself every year, even to prices, which, given certain Latin American inflation rates, can change out of all recognition. (The price of a rented hammock at the Mayan ruins of Tikal is still fifty cents, however.) Taking each country in turn, the *Handbook* moves pyramidally from the general to the particular: from geographical and historical summations to regions, cities, towns, and even villages, from current economic reports to a concluding section of brisk practical information on matters like money, travel, documents, food, dress, and national habits, sufficient to allay the anxieties of even the most timorous.

The pleasure one takes in reading the *Handbook* is that of feeling the huge, unwieldy abstractions of the Latin American countries reduced to a sharply observed particularity, as though they had been trudged through by someone in no hurry at all, and taken in by a kindly, unjudging, sympathetic eye. It has none of the lapel-tugging tone of those trailblazing guides written for tourists, and treats its readers, instead, as travelers who are out to see and absorb. It proffers its occasional advice with a nannylike, finger-wagging directness, even reminding us where certain church services are conducted in English. But it will quite often turn either wry or lyrical where the circumstance seems to demand it.

Soaked in attention, the little crowded capsule of the *Handbook* swells into a whole continent of information. I cannot think of any better way of illustrating the arbitrary richness of this prodigious vade mecum than by stitching together a random patchwork of some of its entries, ranging from the blunt to the exotic. Sanity is its keynote, and its temper remains unruffled in the face of the most improbable trials:

> Be careful when asking directions. Many Latin Americans will give you the wrong answer rather than admit they do not know; this may be partly because they fear losing face, but is also because they like to please!

But the dry editorial smile is never too far from the surface:

> Chagas' Disease (South American Trypanosomiasis) is a chronic illness, incurable, transmitted by the 'barber bug', which lives in rural districts on dirt floors frequented by opossums. It bites at night so avoid sleeping in such conditions.

> If you are unlucky enough to be bitten by a venomous snake, spider, scorpion or sea creature, always try (within limits) to catch the animal for identification.

> In reply to our 1972 statement that some State Tourist Hotels [in Peru] find the proper tariff too difficult to calculate and charge a blanket 12%, the Tourist Department emphatically deny that there is any surcharge for extra blankets at any of their hotels.

In this Sierra in Colombia live the Motilones Indians. A connoisseur of the ironies of history will know that at the Congress of El Rosario one of the items most acclaimed was the admission of aboriginal Indians into citizenship. The Motilones have always turned a blind eye to this, for they are the only Indians in Colombia who have refused to accept the inevitable. Little is known of them, for so far they have persisted in killing many of the missionaries sent to Christianise them, and the anthropologists sent to study them.

The great achievement of the *Handbook* – and it comes largely from the practice of using the material sent in by enthusiastic travelers – is that of bringing Latin America into the focus of individual perception. Entries like the following have a certain endearing practicality to them:

> On the Bolivian side, in Lake Huanamarca, i.e. from Straits of Tiquina south, the best way to visit the Lake from La Paz is to take from Avenida Buenos Aires a bus to Huatajata and there ask for Nicolás Catari. He is a great boat-builder and knows the Lake well.

Similarly:

> If the Bolivian Immigration Officer at Villazón is not in his office, you can ask for him at Hotel Panamericano, just up from the Post Office.

Its practicality is often laconically direct:

> 1st class US$4.50, 2nd US$2.50, no apparent difference.

Clearly, the *Handbook* has the traveler's welfare at heart, warning like a wise uncle against pitfalls and pickpockets, but without any pious moralising:

> During the new year's fiesta [in Pasto, Colombia] there is a 'Día de los Negros' on Jan. 5 and a 'Día de los Blancos' next day. On 'black day' people dump their hands in black grease and paint, without exception, each other's faces black. On 'white day' they throw talc or flour at each other. Local people wear their oldest

clothes. Things can get quite violent. On December 28 and Feb. 5, there is also a 'Fiesta de las Aguas' when anything that moves – only tourists, because locals know better – gets drenched with water from balconies and even from fire engines' hoses.

Visitors should know – for their own good – that a thriving industry in Quito is the production of religious paintings of a medieval type. And another is the stealthy sale by dubious chaps of shrunken heads (*tsantsa*), war trophies of the Jivaro head-hunters. Nowadays they are fakes made out of goatskin, their long black hair making them look very like the real thing.

I was able to test the following advice, and, in consequence, I would never dream of ignoring the *Handbook's* counsel:

On the night ferry to Montevideo rush to the dining place if you want to spare yourself a supperless night.

And think of the difference the following information makes to a traveler in the Centrál Cordillera region of Colombia:

The gardens, and even the stations, are bright with flowers. The track, however, leaves much to be desired and always seems to be under repair; the journey by rail takes 24 hours whereas buses do it in seven.

I find myself hoping that the countries in question take heed of the *Handbook,* for they might be able to do something about a comment like this:

You need to have your own shoe-cleaning equipment; there seem to be no shoeshine boys in any of the Guianas!

And my favorite warning of all, which must make anyone wary of ever opening his mouth in Guatemala:

Watch out for would-be guides in Antigua who engage you in friendly conversation and then charge you US$3 for the privilege.

It is impossible to wander in the *Handbook* without amassing a treasury of miscellaneous information, which is usually delivered as a murmured aside:

In Potosí, Bolivia, immense amounts of silver were once extracted from this hill. In Spain, '*éste es un Potosí*' ('it's a Potosí') is still used for anything superlatively rich.

In Gualeguay, Argentina:

The house from whose ridgepole Garibaldi was hung by one hand and tortured by the local chief of police in 1837, in the time of Rosas, still exists,

And a rich nugget of information about Nevis, in the Leeward Islands:

Here Nelson met and married Frances Nesbit; the Nesbit plantation still exists today and is a guest house open all the year round (US$40 single MAP). Here, too, was born Alexander Hamilton, who helped to draft the American Constitution. The former capital, Jamestown, was drowned by a tidal wave in 1680. The submerged town can still be visited by snorkelers and skindivers and, according to the locals, the tolling of its church bells can still be heard.

It is, however, the occasional sentences cropping up suddenly in the brisk summations of landscapes and small towns which will startle a scene or an atmosphere into being, scattered like jewels in the text and reading as though they might have fallen from the prose of some of the Latin American novelists:

Vultures still stalk the streets like turkeys.

The ruins are vestigial; the cacti are far more interesting.

Now and then the drab, depressing landscape is brightened by the red poncho of an Indian shepherd watching his sheep.

From there, is a road through Panzós to Tactic, which is famous for beautiful *huipiles* and for its 'living well', in which the water becomes agitated as one approaches.

The streets, steep, twisted and narrow, follow the contour of the hills and are sometimes steps cut into the rock: one, the Street of the Kiss, is so narrow that kisses can be – and are – exchanged from opposite balconies.

West of Tandil stood the famous balancing stone called the Piedra Movediza; it fell of its own accord in 1912. Whilst it stood, the huge mass of granite was so exquisitely balanced that light puffs of wind would set it swaying. Indians in the last century believed the stone would fall as a sign of God's approbation if white men were driven out of the country. General Rosas ordered the stone to be pulled down, but a number of men hauling away with oxen teams failed to dislodge it.

A large number of Indians are met on the road: peripatetic merchants laden with goods, or villagers driving pigs to market, or women carrying babies and cockerels and fruits. Your driver can usually tell from their costumes where they come from. The merchant will often do a round of 200 km. and make no more than a dollar or two, but he likes wandering, the contacts with strange people and the novel sights. He pleases himself, pleases his customers and . . . is not much concerned whether he can make pleasure pay.

One has to be grateful for good guidebooks – their compressed experience saves a lot of time. Wandering about in Latin America with the comfortable bulk of *The South American Handbook* has led me to feel the greatest possible respect for its English good sense, its crisp practicality, its gentle curiosity. It is English, too, in its political imperviousness: whatever horrors and injustices may be enacted in these territories, the territories are at least there.

Borges and Neruda

When I first went to Spain, in 1953, I knew little about the living country and barely a word of the language. But my senses were in good working order, and I was instantly drawn in by Spain's rhythms and its landscapes – the burned, sun-stained earth, the silver-blue clarity of Mediterranean light, the warm solemnity of the people, the spareness of village life. Existence was honed down to its essentials, making the days longer, time more abundant. So I returned to Spain, and returned, and eventually went to live there in 1956, setting out to learn the country, and slowly absorb the Spanish sense of time. Spaniards have a gift for expanding the present, around a meal or a conversation; and they are masters of the cosmic shrug that sheds all preoccupations except those immediately at hand. But living in Spain meant, above all, entering the Spanish language, for in those early days I felt separated from the spoken life around me, a bafflement hard to bear. Spanish, at first encounter, is welcoming: you enter it by way of the market and the kitchen, but you soon find yourself stranded on that plateau of daily needs. The language lies still beyond. Living in another language means growing another self, and it takes time for that other self to become a familiar. While I went about learning the machinery and the music, I realised at the same time that the Spanish I was acquiring was as devoid of context as that of a young child, for I had no past in the language. I was lucky, however, in having wise friends, and, following their counsel, I entered a continuum of reading and listening.

There is nothing like immersion in an unknown – new places, new landscapes, new preoccupations, new loves, a new language – to sharpen the edge of attention. From Majorca, where I first landed, I moved to Madrid and then to Barcelona. I travelled all over – to the Basque country, to Andalusia, to Gibraltar and Morocco, to Portugal – looking and listening a lot, and I wrote the first of a series of chronicles on Spain for *The New Yorker*. Soon after it appeared, I had my Spanish press credentials withdrawn, but that made little difference, for Spain existed then on rumour and speculation. Living there felt like belonging to an extensive whispered conspiracy against the Franco regime. Spain was at something of a standstill, still in shock from the Civil War and the long isolation that followed it, threadbare compared to the rest of Europe. Censorship, both moral and political, hung heavy over the press, over the universities, and over writers and publishers, and the police had sharp antennae out for any sign of dissidence. The writers I knew complained that years of censorship had instilled in Spaniards the habit of censoring themselves. Newspapers were grey and evasive, written opinion was sparse and guarded, and literature was thin and spare.

Among my friends in Barcelona was a young poet and publisher named Carlos Barral, lean, birdlike, throaty-voiced, and given to infectious enthusiasms. Carlos's imprint, Seix Barral, published the work of new Spanish writers and of European writers in translation, and consequently was always battling the censor. Carlos's enthusiasm at that time, however, was for the writing that was beginning to appear from the countries of Spanish America. In 1962, he published Mario Vargas Llosa's novel *La Ciudad y los Perros*, later translated as *The Time of the Hero*. The book was received in Spain with an excitement hardly ever generated by the Spanish novels of the day, and it led Carlos to proclaim, with remarkable prescience, that it was from the countries of Spanish America that we should expect not just the next literary flowering but the renewing of the Spanish language.

In those days, the attitude of Spaniards toward Spanish America most resembled the way the English used to regard the United States, with an insufferable condescension. Europe was much more immediate to them than the South American continent, and their knowledge of it was vague. So was mine. I had in my head a mixture of school geography, Hollywood epics, Carmen Miranda with fruit on her head, paeons asleep under huge sombreros, the bossa nova, and the chachacha. It may have had something to do with the stasis of Spain at the time, but, through the books and manuscripts that Carlos passed on to me – books like Juan Rulfo's *Pedro Páramo* and Alejo Carpentier's *The Lost Steps* – I began to take an impassioned interest in South America, and to read its turbulent history with some amazement. More than that, I found in the literature a loosening of Spanish from its Castilian restraints, an intense verbal energy. I noticed the same thing in the few Spanish Americans I came across in Barcelona: they had more exuberance than we were used to in Spain and, given the occasion, they turned conversation on its ear, making a playground of the language.

When Mario Vargas Llosa came to Barcelona, Carlos introduced me. Mario had left Peru behind and lived in Paris, working for the French radio network: he broadcast to Latin America at night and wrote by day. He had a kind of flashing intensity to him, and a single, burning ambition: to live by his writing. It was nearly impossible, he said, to make a living as a writer in Latin America: editions were small, readers were sparse, and few writers were read beyond their own borders, since tariff barriers in many countries made books hard to come by. While the separate countries of Latin America all had their writers, it made little sense, Mario said, to speak of a 'Latin American' literature. As yet, there was no body of writing that had found its way through translation into other literatures and so achieved international recognition. Within a decade, that was to change utterly, with the surge of memorable novels, popularly referred to as the Boom, that appeared in the aftermath of the Cuban Revolution of 1959 and received great acclaim in many languages: novels by Vargas Llosa, Julio Cortázar, Gabriel García Márquez, José Donoso, Alejo Carpentier, and Guillermo Cabrera Infante. Prior to that eruption, however, very few writers from Spanish America had earned international attention. Foremost among them were the Chilean poet Pablo Neruda and the Argentine master Jorge Luis Borges. They were, each in a quite separate way, the forerunners of the writers of the Boom.

I had been introduced to Borges's writing a few years earlier, by Pipina Prieto, a vivacious Argentine who had known him in Buenos Aires and who spoke of him with such fervour that when she pressed his *Ficciones* on me I would not have dared not read it. The effect on an unsuspecting reader of encountering a work of Borges's can be alarming enough almost to justify a publisher's warning on the book jacket. His stories induce a kind of vertigo in his readers, an eerie after-effect that can invest small happenings, like breaking a glass or missing a train, with ominous significance. Pipina was a bewitching talker, and could practically perform Borges's stories. We talked them over, endlessly, and before long I kept the half-dozen slender books that contained most of his writing then – poems and essays as well as stories – always at hand.

I had been coming across the poetry of Neruda piecemeal, mostly in the houses of friends, for Neruda's books were then proscribed in Spain as Communist literature. There is an extraordinary lift that comes from reading Neruda's poetry for the first time: both from its sheer beauty on the ear and from its great tumble of images. But I found not one but many Nerudas. I read his fierce elegies on the Spanish Civil War, and his tender, whimsical 'Ode to My Socks', his sensual love poems, and the high incantatory pitch of his *Heights of Machu Picchu*, and I wondered at their accomplished variety but had no sense, yet, of who the poet was among so many incarnations.

That these two writers should be acclaimed as the quintessential Spanish-American writers of their time was particularly intriguing to me, for the more I read them the more I felt them to be about as different from each other, as writers and as human souls, as it is possible to be. Borges's work is as spare as Neruda's is ebullient, as dubious and ironic as Neruda's is passionately affirmative, as reticent as Neruda's is voluble. Where Neruda is open, even naïve, Borges is oblique and sceptical; where Neruda is a sensualist, a poet of physical love, a man of appetites, Borges is an ascetic; where Neruda is rooted in what he has experienced, Borges seems to have lived almost entirely in literature, in the mind-travel of his reading. Borges accepted being Argentine as his destiny, Buenos Aires as his locality, but his preoccupations were wholly meta-physical. Where Neruda in his poems addressed the realities of the Latin-American present and lived on intimate terms with the physical world, Borges's writings often cast doubt on the very existence of that world, except as a mental projection, a fiction.

★

Borges was born in 1899, in the Buenos Aires suburb of Palermo, into a middle-class professional family: his father was a lawyer and a teacher of psychology with literary aspirations, his mother a descendant of military heroes and Argentine patriots. From an early age, the son was seen by the family as destined to become a writer, fulfilling the ambitions of his father, whose literary career had been stayed by encroaching blindness – a hereditary blindness, which was to descend on Borges gradually from his late twenties. In 1914, the whole family moved to Europe, where they lived for the next seven years – first in Geneva, where Borges studied and read French and German, and then in Spain, where he began to write in earnest. When he returned to Argentina, in 1921, fired by a new enthusiasm for his country, he began a literary career – as a poet, an essayist, and a reviewer, in the world of salons, *tertulias*, and small magazines – that continued all his life.

Neruda had his beginnings in 1904, in Parral, in the rainy south of Chile, where his father worked on the railroad, on the frontier of the great forests. He has recreated his solitary, awestruck childhood, his discovery of the secret life of words, in a number of enchanted poems. Luck seemed to attend him early. His first poems were brought to the attention of the Chilean poet Gabriela Mistral, and she helped him gain a scholarship to study French in Santiago when he was seventeen. In the capital, he moved from the absorbed solitude of adolescence into an artist's underworld of close friendships, nightlong conversations, sexual love, and the poems of Rimbaud and Baudelaire. It was a heady transformation. Neruda's *Twenty Love Poems and a Song of Despair*, published in 1924 (written in that flush of late adolescence), became, and still are, a kind of touchstone for first love, learned by heart everywhere in the Spanish-speaking world. 'I have been marking the blank chart of your body,' Neruda writes in one of them, 'with crosses of fire / My mouth was a spider that scuttles into hiding / In you, behind you, tremulous and thirsty.' These poems are remarkable in their erotic intensity, in their startling sensual directness.

Such early fame led to Neruda's being appointed, in that most enlightened of Latin-American traditions, to the Chilean Consular Service, and between the ages of twenty-three and twenty-eight he was posted in turn to Rangoon, Ceylon, Java, and Singapore. The five years Neruda was away from Chile were a difficult time for him, separated from his language and his roots; yet out of his loneliness and alienation came the cumulative volumes of *Residencia en la Tierra* (*Sojourn on Earth*) — hallucinatory poems in which, deprived of his own country, he creates wildly surreal landscapes out of his own private obsessions, with a poetic density quite startlingly new to poetry in Spanish. When he returned to Chile, his fame as a poet had spread so widely that, posted to Spain in 1934, he was acclaimed by the community of Spanish poets, Federico García Lorca and Miguel Hernández among them. But these were the last euphoric days of the Republic. When the Civil War broke out, Neruda remained in Spain, but the experience marked him forever. His friend García Lorca was sought out and shot, and everywhere about him Neruda saw Spain broken. The war brought about in him a deep political conversion. He was asked to resign his consulship because of his outspoken sympathy for the Republic. The poems he wrote at that time are bitter in their anger.

> Generals,
> traitors,
> look at my dead house,
> look at broken Spain:
> out of every dead house comes burning metal
> instead of flowers,
> out of every crater in Spain
> Spain reappears,
> out of every dead child comes a rifle with eyes,
> every crime breeds bullets
> that will one day find their way
> to your heart.
>
> You will ask why don't his poems
> tell us of dreams, of leaves,
> of the great volcanoes of his homeland?

Come and see the blood in the streets.
come and see
the blood in the streets,
come and see the blood
in the streets!

Back in Chile, Neruda, still haunted by his Spanish experience, joined the Chilean Communist Party, and in 1945 was elected to the Chilean Senate, plunging into an active political life. After he published, in 1947, an open letter criticising President Gabriel González Videla, he was forced into hiding for an extended period to avoid arrest, and was sheltered in different houses until he could escape over the Andes to Argentina. Out of that came his *Canto General*, an enormous hymn to Latin America – its exotic geography, its cruel history, its brutal politics, and its present human wrongs – in a sprawling mass of poems. The book, published in 1950, had an immense impact, more political than poetic. Besides the overtly political poems, however, it contained a sequence of visionary cantos he called *Alturas de Macchu Picchu* (*The Heights of Macchu Picchu*). He had visited the Inca shrine in 1943, and these impassioned invocations contain Neruda's poetic creed. He sees Macchu Picchu as built on the bones of centuries of oppressed Indians, and he vows to become a voice for all things that have no voice, to speak out for the oppressed of the past and against the oppressions of the present. In this new writing, Neruda abandoned the surreal extravagance of his earlier work, and thenceforth deliberately simplified his poetry, to make it accessible to the people of Chile who gave him shelter in their houses as a fugitive. In Chile, he was now a national possession.

*

Alongside such a crowded existence, Borges's life appears singularly static. On his return to Buenos Aires from Europe, he set about rediscovering his native city, first in poems and then in a series of incisive essays on Argentine themes. His world was a purely literary one; he regularly reviewed foreign literature, and translated works of Virginia Woolf, Kafka, Joyce, and Faulkner into Spanish. But his brief literary essays were often oblique and unconventional: with time, a certain playful element showed itself – in quotations ascribed to nonexistent originals, citations of imaginary authors. Although Borges was not writing fiction, he began to intrude fictional elements into his other writings. He used to say that he considered scholarship merely a branch of fantastic literature. He told me once that as a young man he had contemplated writing a long dynastic novel encompassing the history of Argentina since independence, until he realised that he could write, in the span of a few pages, a descriptive review of just such a work by an invented author, adding his reflections on the genre. It was not until 1939, following first the death of his father and then a long convalescence after a near-fatal accident, that he began to write the disquieting stories that were published in 1944 as *Ficciones* – the stories that brought him fame far beyond Argentina.

It is somewhat deceptive to talk of Borges as a storyteller, as a poet, or as an essayist, however, for he blurred these divisions by exploring the same paradoxes in the varying forms of story, poem, and essay. To him they are all 'fictions' – words on a page, constructs of the mind. Borges concludes his epilogue to *El Hacedor*, a collection he published in 1960, with the following:

A man sets himself the task of drawing the world.

As the years pass, he fills the empty space with images of provinces and kingdoms, mountains, bays, ships, islands, fish, houses, instruments, stars, horses, and people. Just before he dies, he discovers that the patient labyrinth of lines traces the image of his own face.

Such fictions are Borges's trademark. From the sixties on, Borges's reputation spread with the speed of a virus through the reading world, infecting it with a sly, humorous scepticism about language, about all matters literary. His writings are deeply subversive – by implication, they call into question all linguistic versions of everything. In whatever Borges writes he never lets his readers forget that what they hold in their hands is a text, a fiction made of words, from a fallible mind. The natural world remains fearful and incomprehensible to us; to contend with it, to give it order and purpose, the mind creates fictions – fables, histories, rules, codes of law, theories, social systems, predictions, even divinities. However 'perfect' these fictions might be, reality defies them by remaining chaotic and unpredictable. Yet the making of fictions is essential to our nature: literature, Borges insists, is our solace.

In 1961, Borges shared with Samuel Beckett the Prix International des Éditeurs, which led to immediate translation of his stories into the main European languages. Anthony Kerrigan, who was editing Ficciones in English, asked me to translate the story 'Tlön, Uqbar, Orbis Tertius'. By then, I had come to know and appreciate Borges's uncharacteristic prose style – a style that is spare, restrained, and carefully formal, and uses something like understatement, not exactly a characteristic of written Spanish. While I worked I had the curious feeling that I was retranslating something back into English that had previously been translated into Spanish. Most crucial to me was to catch the tone – tentative, wary, uncertain – in which Borges writes, a manner that constantly questions what it is telling, sometimes by tone alone.

'Tlön, Uqbar, Orbis Tertius' begins with Borges's discovery, through a chance remark by a friend, of an item in a corrupt encyclopedia about an enigmatic region called Uqbar. The region is apparently fictitious. 'Reading it over,' Borges says characteristically, 'we discovered, beneath the superficial authority of the prose, a fundamental vagueness.' Some time later, in a remote hotel, chance puts into Borges's hands a volume of another encyclopedia, devoted to a vast planet called Tlön. A trail of further clues reveals that a group of seventeenth-century sages originally conceived the idea of creating an entirely rational planet – one that would be wholly comprehensible to its inhabitants – and of disseminating knowledge of it by way of a secret encyclopedia. A postscript to the story, set at a future date, describes how the human race eventually embraces the world of Tlön as though it were reality. Objects from Tlön begin to turn up in the real world, and, as in many of Borges's stories, reality gives way to a wished-for fiction.

For Borges, rational systems that are extended to the extreme limits of their rationality turn into nightmare. In his 'The Library of Babel', a 'total' library is obliged to contain not only all actual books but all possible books as well. The entire world becomes a library. In 'The Babylon Lottery', set in an imagined past of Babylon, an apparently rational society elects to introduce some element of chance into its existence by starting a lottery. Bit by bit, to increase the excitement, the numbers of the lottery are made to signify not just prizes but punishments – fines, imprisonment, even execution. The mysterious company administering the lottery is eventually suspected of being a fiction. Babylon gives itself over completely to chance, and order yields irresistibly to chaos.

★

Neruda and Borges met only once, in July of 1927, in Buenos Aires. Following the success of *Twenty Love Poems*, Neruda, then turning twenty-three, was on his way to take up his first diplomatic appointment, as Chilean consul in Rangoon. Borges, at twenty-seven, had published two volumes of poems and was an active reviewer in the literary magazines of the day. The meeting was one that each of them described in later life: they recalled that they had talked about the unsatisfactory nature of Spanish, and the resignation they both felt at having to write in it. The one enthusiasm they shared was for the poems of Walt Whitman, whose work both of them had translated. The meeting appears to have been more diplomatic than intimate, and they went to some trouble to avoid meeting again. It seems to have occurred to each of them that they had little in common as writers except the Spanish language; as time went on, they were often asked about each other, and in their responses they were most of the time polite and respectful, no more. Borges regarded their meeting as essentially nonserious. Neruda was more specific. In a letter to an Argentine friend he wrote:

> Borges, whom you mention, seems to me over-preoccupied with those problems of culture and society which do not attract me, which are not human. I prefer the great wines, love, suffering, and books as a consolation for the inevitable solitude. I even feel a certain scorn for culture as a way of interpreting things. I prefer,

sure awareness without precedent, a physical absorption in the world . . . History, the problems of 'knowledge', as they are called, seem to me lacking in dimension. How much of it would it take to fill the void? I see around me always fewer ideas, always more bodies, sunshine and sweat. I am exhausted.

For all their youthful excess, Neruda's observations, about himself in particular, are remarkably clear. He remained entirely a poet of the physical world, a materialist, actually as well as politically: he had no interest in metaphysical questions, and disliked literary talk. He did not write his poems for literary circles: he wanted them out in the street, read by everyday inhabitants of the language. He achieved just that, in his own time, as has no other poet I can think of. He accomplished what Whitman only aspired to; he became what Whitman had hoped to be.

Borges, on the other hand, remained remote, indecipherable to many: it requires a certain nerve even to try to follow the quirks of his mind. In a celebrated essay, 'Kafka and His Precursors', he makes the point that after reading Kafka we recognise foreshadowings of him in the work of writers who preceded him in time, and we refer to them as Kafkaesque. As Borges wrote, 'The fact is that every writer creates his own precursors. His work modifies our conception of the past, as it will modify the future.' This is precisely what has happened in Borges's case. Certain intrusions of disquiet that undermine a believed reality are so much a mark of his mind and manner that when we find the same dismaying twists in writers who preceded him in time we refer to these twists as Borgesian.

It may well have been the intense appeal of Borges's writings to academics in all languages that made him such an intrusive literary figure. Books about him abound, theses and critical studies multiply: unravelling Borges is something of an industry. Neruda, to the contrary, has attracted comparatively little critical study: the great mass of his poetry is simply there, always accessible, like the ocean.

★

The more I read my way into Spanish America, the more I felt my ignorance of it as a living place. When a piece of time suddenly opened for me in early 1964, I bought a round-trip ticket from New York to Buenos Aires that allowed me an unlimited number of linear stops. I made many. I met a whole web of writers, and they passed me on from one country to friends in the next. I made solitary pilgrimages to shrines like Chichen Itzá and Machu Picchu, but otherwise, wherever I went, I found myself in the middle of a seemingly endless conversation that ranged all the way from pure play to high art. I asked a lot of questions, but mostly I listened.

In mid-February, I landed into a golden summer in Chile. Someone had given me a letter to Jorge Elliot, a painter and art critic in Santiago, and I called on him soon after arriving. He welcomed me as though I had been expected, and invited me to a summer house he had in Isla Negra, the village on the Pacific Coast where Neruda then lived.

Isla Negra was little more than a string of houses built along a low cliff above a broad beach where the Pacific thundered incessantly. The families who lived there knew each other well, and the place had a well-worn, easygoing air. Neruda had settled there in the fifties, in a house perched on the cliff, and he had added to it eccentrically as money came in, book by book. Beside the house stood a ship's yardarm, and as we approached it Jorge pointed out a small blue flag flying from it. 'Pablo's at home,' he said.

Neruda's garden was dominated by a steamroller that he had rescued, painted, and installed as a shrine. Under the yardarm, a boat was grounded, geraniums growing from its stem, and beyond it lay an anchor, all of them like props from Neruda's poems. We went inside, and into a high-ceilinged living room with stone walls, a fireplace framed by granite boulders from the beach, and a wooden gallery with stairs descending. Objects were everywhere: ships' figureheads leaning out of the corners; driftwood; shells; tackle; books. On a long, heavy table under a wide window that framed the Pacific lay more objects: a ship under glass; a sextant; a telescope; odd-shaped bottles; agates gathered from the beach. The light in the room wavered with the white of the breaking waves below. The house might have been afloat. Suddenly, Neruda called out, and came down from the gallery, a captain descending from his bridge.

He was a large man – portly, even – but majestic and deliberate in his movement. His eyes were large and hooded, rather like those of a bemused lizard, and seemed to take in everything, but slowly. He moved slowly, turned his head slowly, blinked slowly; and when he spoke his voice, mellowly resonant, was close to languid. His words had the weight of stones. I noticed, then and whenever I later met him, that, since he was generally the centre of attention, he had a way of slowing down everything around him, pacing the conversation. As he talked, he moved about the room, touching a surface here, picking up an agate from the table and gazing into it, entranced. The objects were a kind of vocabulary: the collections of shells, of ships in bottles, of French postcards, of clocks and hats and walking sticks; a huge wooden shoe he had badgered from a bootmaker; a full-sized papier-mâché horse.

Thinking of Neruda, I still see him in that house: it was an externalisation of his whole being. He used to say that he had a secondary profession, as a surreal architect, a transformer of houses. He required of his houses that they be in remarkable places, that they have space for all the multifarious objects he brought back from his travels, that they have a workroom for his writing, and that they be comfortable, humorous, and accessible to his friends. Each house was his private theatre, where he had designed the sets and always played the lead.

Neruda was then in his sixtieth year, and, in anticipation of his birthday, he had written *Memorial de Isla Negra*, an autobiography in the form of more than a hundred poems, divided into five sections, each covering a stage of his life. The galley proofs were draped along the back of a sofa. He was also translating *Romeo and Juliet* for performance later that year, and he asked me several questions about the text. Neruda was glum about his translation; English and Spanish did such different things, he said, they were really misfits. After some translation tinkering, we moved outside, to a long table adjoining the kitchen, where Neruda's wife, Matilde Urrutia, came to join us.

In the presence of food and drink, Neruda always expanded visibly. On this occasion, he brought the sheaf of galleys to the table, and at a replete pause he read to us, in that mesmerising voice, carefully phrased, that seemed to float the poem in the air. I had no inkling of it then, but seventeen years later I was to translate that book in its entirety, poem by poem.

Later that night, I talked with Jorge about Neruda. He found for me a copy of Neruda's brief prose manifesto *On Impure Poetry*.

It is very appropriate, at certain times of the day or night, to look deeply into objects at rest: wheels which have traversed vast dusty spaces, bearing great cargoes of vegetables or minerals, sacks from the coal yards, barrels, baskets, the handles and grips of the carpenter's tools. They exude the touch of man and the earth as a lesson to the tormented poet. Worn surfaces, the mark hands have left on things, the aura, sometimes tragic and always wistful, of these objects lend to reality a fascination not to be taken lightly.

The flawed confusion of human beings shows in them, the proliferation, materials used and discarded, the prints of feet and fingers, the permanent mark of humanity on the inside and outside of all objects.

That is the kind of poetry we should be after, poetry worn away as if by acid by the labour of hands, impregnated with sweat and smoke, smelling of lilies and of urine, splashed by the variety of what we do, legally or illegally.

A poetry as impure as old clothes, as a body, with its foodstains and its shame, with wrinkles, observations, dreams, wakefulness, prophecies, declarations of love and hate, stupidities, shocks, idylls, political beliefs, negations, doubts, affirmations, taxes.

I went back along the sand path to Neruda's house several times. He and I combed the beach for agates at the ebb, laughed a lot, talked a lot, ate and drank exuberantly well. Since I wore no shoes, Pablo and Matilde called me, then and ever after, Patapelá (Barefoot), and when I said my farewells Pablo gave me a volume of his, *Estravagario*. We made promises to meet again, somewhere, sometime. Such a meeting seemed to me improbable; but then so did being in Chile, that long, thin, bountiful country.

When I left, I flew to Mendoza, at the foot of the Andes on the Argentine side, and, with two days to wait for the train across the pampas to Buenos Aires, I made notes and read, Isla Negra still vivid in my head. The trees in Mendoza's elegant small squares were shedding their leaves, and under a limpid blue sky the dark wall of the Andes towered in the piercing clarity of the air. It felt to me like Shangri-La.

*

Buenos Aires has always struck me as the most sumptuous of cities: the abundance of its shops and restaurants made Madrid and Barcelona then seem frugal by comparison, and in its well-stocked bookstores I bought the books forbidden us in Spain – principally Neruda's *Collected Poems*, a Losada volume, on India paper, of a thousand nine hundred and thirty-two pages. Very little of Buenos Aires seemed Spanish. Listening to conversations in that assured *porteño* accent, I felt that the Spanish language had now detached itself from Spain, and had taken on many different modes. After a day or two of exploring, I telephoned Borges at the National Library where he had been director since 1955. Pipina had written ahead to him, and had given me his number.

He came on the line, and, on identifying me, he changed to his very courteous English and asked me to call on him in the library that afternoon. When I arrived, I was directed by a guard to Borges's office. I must have misheard, for I found myself in the deeper twilit recesses of the library, lost. I might almost have expected it. An assistant rescued me and led me to where Borges sat, at the end of a long library table, a pile of books at hand, in a pool of light cast by the lamp. He rose to greet me, his face upturned toward the sound of my voice.

That meeting, the first of many, so imprinted itself on me that each time I met Borges I felt I was reenacting it. It came in part from his blindness, which meant that one had to find one's way to him, a presence, waiting patiently. To exist for him, people had to come within his earshot, into the pool of his attention, a pool that encompassed a library of blind volumes, all of Borges's memory, all he had read and thought, all he had written and would write. To meet him was to be admitted to the universe of his blindness, to the crowded solitude he inhabited, to the still pool of his attention.

There was something frail about his company – the soft, quiet voice, the conceded vulnerability of his blindness. He mostly spoke to me in English, which he had learned as a child from his paternal grandmother, an Englishwoman of Northumbrian stock – Borges's English had a faint northern cast to it. As he explained once in an interview, 'When I was talking to my paternal grandmother I had to speak in a manner that I afterwards discovered was called English, and when I was talking to my mother or her parents I had to talk a language that afterwards turned out to be Spanish.' It was in English that he read first, in his father's library. He thought of English ever after as the language of culture, Spanish as the language his mother spoke in the kitchen to the servants, the language of the street and the outside world. He spoke English with the respect due a language he knew well but did not live in: he spoke in the careful cadence of books. On other occasions, in Spanish-speaking company, he would become much more mischievous, less solemn. Yet I think it was the very fact of his bilingual upbringing that gave him his acute sense of the arbitrary and deceptive nature of language: a bilingual is much more aware of the gulf between word and thing than someone confined to a single language.

Irony accompanied Borges like a familiar, present not only in everything he wrote but also in so many of the circumstances of his life: in the family's understanding that he would become a writer and yet would probably succumb to the congenital blindness that had afflicted his father and five preceding generations; in his appointment as director of the National Library just when he was no longer able to read the volumes he presided over. When we left the library for a walk on the Southside, the Buenos Aires of many of his poems, his one hand lightly in the crook of my arm, his stick ever present in the other, it was I who was seeing the city and reading the street signs, but it was Borges who provided the foot-notes and the anecdotes. Sometimes, invoking a text, he paused as if leafing through a library in his head before finding the book and the page and haltingly bringing back the sentence or the line.

Around Borges in Buenos Aires I sensed a host of attendant spirits – waiters and taxi-drivers who knew his ways, friends ready to read to him or take his dictation, assistants in the library who watched over him – for now that his fame had spread to Europe and the United States he had become a national treasure. Passersby in the street murmured his name as a kind of salutation. I returned him to the library, to the guard who stood by the door. We said our goodbyes, and I moved out of the circle of his attention into the labyrinth of that inexhaustible city, of which he once wrote:

> Hard to believe Buenos Aires had any beginning.
> I feel it to be as eternal as air and water.

Although I then spent some days in Brazil, I realised that I had reached a kind of saturation, that I had enough to occupy my mind for a foreseeable time. So I made my way, by stages, back to Spain, where I unpacked my book hoard. In the late seventies, I was to do the reverse: pack and send books from the newly democratic Spain to friends in Chile and Argentina, both then in political darkness.

★

But at this time it was Spain that had become politically uncomfortable, and in late 1966 I returned to Britain, moving to London with my son, Jasper, to live for the next three years on a houseboat on the Thames at Chelsea Reach. Fastened to London only by our mooring, we felt ourselves to be something of an offshore island. We found many Latin American friends in London at that time, Mario Vargas Llosa and Guillermo Cabrera Infante among them. Sometimes the boat sounded like a Spanish American outpost moored to the Chelsea Embankment.

Earlier that year, I had met Emir Rodriguez Monegal, a long-time friend and chronicler of both Borges and Neruda. Emir – dark, sharp-faced, incisive, and with great charm – had just been appointed director of a new cultural review called *Mundo Nuevo*, which he edited from Paris. Emir came to England once a week to give a seminar at Cambridge, and regularly stopped off at the houseboat on the way. A prodigious and perceptive reader, he had realised that, at that particular moment in the countries of Spanish America, a number of extraordinary writers were surfacing, and that all at once a Latin American literature was coming into being, more than fulfilling the prediction that Carlos Barral had made in Barcelona. *Mundo Nuevo*, which, under Monegal, ran to just twenty-five issues, is often credited with having launched the Boom. Emir published the work of Cabrera Infante, the brilliant Cuban writer who had just then sought political asylum in London, as well as the first fragment of García Márquez's *One Hundred Years of Solitude*. García Márquez was politically in sympathy with Neruda, and revered him as a poet, yet his book also shows everywhere the influence of Borges – in how it regards odd and magical happenings as natural events, and sees everywhere the collisions between private fictions and an unyielding reality.

The shadows of Neruda and Borges hung over the whole generation of writers that followed them – not so much as direct literary influences but as forerunners. Neruda held out his vision of a South American *continent*, sharing a turbulent history, a singular humanity, and a common plight. Borges swept away the previous restraints of realism by demonstrating that fiction creates a separate world, where a writer can make his own laws and create his own appropriate language. While Spanish America's younger writers mostly took their passion and politics from Neruda, it was Borges who reminded them of the magical nature of their craft. Emir once suggested to me that, just as Don Quixote and Sancho Panza, seen as sides of the same person, reflect the contradictions of the Spanish character, so the Spanish American psyche could be thought of as embracing the sensual immediacy of Neruda and the labyrinthine questionings of Borges.

Borges and Neruda gave extensive interviews to Rita Guibert for a book she published in 1973 on Latin American writers. Of Borges's politics Neruda had this to say: 'If he thinks like a dinosaur, that has nothing to do with my thinking. He doesn't understand a thing about what's happening in the modern world, and he thinks that I don't either. Therefore, we are in agreement.' When Borges was questioned on his politics, he answered this way:

My only commitment is to literature and my own sincerity. As for my political attitude, I've always made it perfectly clear: I've been anti-communist, anti-Hitler, anti-Peronist, and antinationalist . . . If a story or a poem of mine is successful, its success springs from a deeper source than my political views, which may be erroneous and are dictated by circumstances. In my case, my knowledge of what is called political reality is very incomplete. My life is really spent among books, many of them from a past age.

For Borges, an intellectual anarchist, politics took place in the street, not in his mind, yet he was not untouched by them. His family, professional and middle-class, traditionally voted conservative, and when the Second World War broke out they were emphatically pro-British. In 1946, Borges had made known in print his opposition to Juan Perón's dictatorship, which he saw as pro-Axis. He was dismissed from his post in a municipal library and appointed poultry inspector in a public market, a post he never filled but a humiliation he never forgot. The military government that succeeded Perón, in 1955, made amends by appointing Borges the director of the National Library, which was tantamount to appointing him the national touchstone he became.

★

From the sixties on, I translated a fair part of Borges's poetry for various selections of his work; and I collaborated in an edition of Neruda's *Selected Poems*, going on later to translate several single volumes of his. Translating someone's work, poetry in particular, has something about it akin to being possessed, haunted. Translating a poem means not only reading it deeply and deciphering it but clambering about backstage among the props and the scaffolding. I found I could no longer read a poem of Neruda's simply as words on a page without hearing behind them that languid, caressing voice. Most important to me in translating these two writers was the sound of their voices in my memory, for it very much helped in finding the English appropriate to those voices. I found that if I learned poems of Neruda's by heart I could replay them at odd moments, on buses, at wakeful times in the night, until, at a certain point, the translation would somehow set. The voice was the clue: I felt that all Neruda's poems were fundamentally vocative – spoken poems, poems of direct address – and that Neruda's voice was in a sense the instrument for which he wrote. He once made a tape for me, reading pieces of different poems, in different tones and rhythms. I played it over so many times that I can hear it in my head at will. Two lines of his I used to repeat like a Zen koan, for they seemed to apply particularly to translating:

> in this net it's not just the strings that count
> but also the air that escapes through the meshes.

He often wrote of himself as having many selves, just as he had left behind him several very different poetic manners and voices. In talking to Rita Guibert, he explained his protean nature thus: 'If my poetry has any virtue it's that it's an organism, it's organic and emanates from my own body. When I was a child, my poetry was childish, it was youthful when I was young, despairing when I was suffering, aggressive when I had to take part in the social struggle, and there is still a mixture of all these different tendencies in the poetry I write now, which may perhaps be at the same time childish, aggressive, and despairing . . . I have always written from some inner necessity . . . I'm an anti-intellectual, I don't much care for analysis or for examining literary currents, and I'm not a writer who subsists on books, although books are necessary to my life.' His dutiful political poems are mainly forgettable, but occasionally the politics and the poetry come together, as in his meditation on food and hunger, 'The Great Tablecloth', which concludes:

> Let us sit down soon to eat
> with all those who haven't eaten,
> let us spread great tablecloths,
> put salt in the lakes of the world,
> set up planetary bakeries,
> tables with strawberries in snow,
> and a plate like the moon itself
> from which we will all eat.
>
> For now I ask no more
> than the justice of eating.

There is so much of Neruda in that single last couplet.

Then I would turn to the universe of Borges. Bringing his poetry into English was much more straightforward. Borges made constant use of certain English verse forms – rhymed quatrains and sonnets in particular – so that translating them required mainly a good ear and a certain prosodic agility in English. In the case of his sonnets, I was careful not to torture them into matching form in English – ingenuity at the expense of poetry. While Neruda's poems are wide-ranging, in their subject matter, their manner, their gesture, their tone, so that they must be taken singly, as separate events, Borges's poems are related to one another, not just in their formal manner and their heraldry of recurring symbols – chessboards, maps, knives, mirrors, coins, labyrinths, tigers, libraries – but in their sceptical, questioning undertone. They let you in on a secret, as observer, as eavesdropper. Translating Borges felt to me like learning a private language: the exact cast of certain favourite words of his, like the noun *olvido*, which he uses to mean either death or sleep or forgetting, and of certain of his vertiginous adjectives, has to be intuited every time. Borges is a much less adventurous or original poet than Neruda: for him, poetry is one of the several dimensions of language he explored, and his poems are mainly parts of a larger whole. He did, however, write a handful of very memorable single poems, like his 'Matthew, XXV:30', in which he imagines a voice confronting him with the vocabulary of his own existence:

> Stars, bread, libraries of East and West,
> playing cards, chessboards, galleries, skylights, cellars,
> a human body to walk with on the earth,
> fingernails, growing at nighttime and in death,
> shadows for forgetting, mirrors that endlessly multiply,
> falls in music, gentlest of all time's shapes,
> borders of Brazil, Uruguay, horses and mornings,
> a bronze weight, a copy of Grettir Saga,
> algebra and fire, the charge at Junín in your blood,
> days more crowded than Balzac, scent of the honeysuckle,
> love, and the imminence of love, and intolerable remembering,

dreams like buried treasure, generous luck,
and memory itself, where a glance can make men dizzy –
all this was given to you and, with it,
the ancient nourishment of heroes –
treachery, defeat, humiliation.
In vain have oceans been squandered on you, in vain
the sun, wonderfully seen through Whitman's eyes.
You have used up the years and they have used up you,
and still, and still, you have not written the poem.

*

Pablo and Matilde turned up in London in 1967, and when Pablo heard that I lived on a houseboat he came straight to inspect it. He decided he must hold his birthday fiesta there, an evening brimming with Chileans, in the course of which a Ukrainian poet had to be rescued from the Thames mud. I accompanied Pablo to the street market in Petticoat Lane and to a ship's chandler by the docks in a vain search for a ship's figurehead. He was anxious to have me translate the whole of *Estravagario*, a favourite book of his, and I agreed with pleasure. In England, wrapped in a Chilean poncho, Pablo looked unnaturally cold, but when we gave a reading together in the Queen Elizabeth Hall I listened to his voice spreading itself like a balm over the English audience – a magical sound, even without the string of sense. After the reading, he was courtesy itself, while regularly casting a side glance in my direction, dinner on his mind.

After being closeted for a spell with the still photographs of his poems, I found it a relief to spend time with the moving original. I knew Neruda much better now, by way of his poems. He was always ready to answer any questions I had about them, even to talk about them, fondly, as about lost friends, but he was not much interested in the mechanics of translation. Once, in Paris, while I was explaining some liberty I had taken, he stopped me and put his hand on my shoulder. 'Alastair, don't just translate my poems. I want you to improve them.'

In 1969, Neruda stood as Communist candidate for the Presidency of Chile, but after a brief campaign he dropped out and threw his support behind his friend Salvador Allende; and Allende, once elected, in 1970, appointed Neruda Chilean Ambassador to France. From then on, Pablo and I saw each other frequently, for he came to London every so often. We had an easy friendship: in his eyes, I, as translator, had joined his cast, and, although he became very much a public poet again, especially following his Nobel Prize in Literature, in 1971, he would shed his official self in the company of friends, as at a backstage party. In the vast Chilean Embassy in Paris, he ignored the voluminous public rooms and furnished a room in his own suite as a French café, with tables, wire chairs, and a zinc bar: it was there that diplomacy, politics, literature, and friendships were all enacted. I had been in Chile in his absence, and, having stayed in his house in Isla Negra, I brought him a full report on the state of the garden and on an extension being built while he was away. Then, late in 1972, he wrote me, saying that he was resigning and returning to Chile. His health had been failing, he explained, and he wanted to be attended to at home. The day of his homecoming was celebrated as a national holiday in Chile, but already, as he had hinted, ominous signs were in the air – not only of Neruda's deteriorating health but of a menacing opposition emerging in Chilean politics. Then, on September II, 1973, the military coup savaged Chile, and twelve days later Neruda died of cancer in a clinic in Santiago. Now only the poems remained. The tape he had made me became, suddenly, like a precious relic, except that I had long since transferred it to my memory, where it never needed rewinding:

> It is time, love, to break off that sombre rose,
> shut up the stars and bury the ash in the earth;
> and, in the rising of the light, wake with those awaking
> or go on in the dream, reaching the other shore of the
>   sea which has no other shore.

While Neruda was running for President in Chile, my son and I were living by the sea on the outskirts of St Andrews in Scotland, and there we received a letter from Borges announcing a forthcoming stop on his way to receive an honorary degree at Oxford. He arrived with Maria Kodama, a graceful, gentle Argentine woman of Japanese ancestry, who acted as his travelling companion, and whom he married, to the gratification of his friends, shortly before he died. He was much affected by being in Scotland, as though his reading had suddenly come to life. He took walks with my son beside the North Sea and pulled Border ballads from his memory. In those few unplanned days, he laid aside the obligation to be Borges, the public self to which his writings bound him, as he described it in his short fiction 'Borges and I':

> I live, I allow myself to live, so that Borges can unwind his writings, and these writings justify me . . . Years ago, I tried to free myself from him and I went from writing down the myths of my district to devising games with time and infinity, but these games have become part of Borges by now, and I will have to think up something else . . . I don't know which of us is writing this page.

One day, a professor saw Borges on the street and, not knowing him, he crossed and addressed him: 'You are Borges, no?' '*A veces*,' Borges replied. 'At times.' By now, Borges was regularly accepting some of the many invitations that came his way – to lecture, to receive honorary degrees and cultural decorations, in Europe and the United States. Reverential audiences came to hear him, as if to confirm that he existed. Once, visiting him in Buenos Aires in 1978, I asked him about his sudden appetite for travel. 'When I am at home in Buenos Aires,' he told me, 'one day is much like another. But when I travel – and you must realise that for me, since I am blind, travelling means merely changing armchairs – friendly ghosts materialise one by one and talk to me about literature, and about my own writings, most generously. For a writer, that is great luxury. I feel blessed by it, I feel lucky.'

Borges had grown tired of lecturing, and when he visited New York, in the late seventies, he would sometimes telephone me and invite me to join him in giving a *charla* – a conversation onstage in which I would ask him questions inviting to his mind. He loved to talk of the hazards of translation: as he once wrote, 'Nothing is as consubstantial with literature and its modest mystery as the questions raised by a translation.' On these occasions, I would sometimes try to surprise him with a question, and as often as not he would surprise me back. I grew to know well a certain movement of his mind, in which he would first make a straightforward statement about a book or a writer and then, after a gravid pause, abruptly undermine it with an ironic afterthought, a subversive aside, mischievous, mocking, desolemnising.

In 1985, in New York, Borges gave me a copy of a recent poem. It had no title, and after some deliberation he decided to call it 'The Web'. It began:

> Which of my cities
> am I doomed to die in?
> Geneva,
> where revelation reached me
> from Virgil and Tacitus?

My translation of the poem lay patiently in *The New Yorker* files until June of 1986, when it saw the light: I received a copy of the magazine while I was in Mexico City. Soon after, coming in from a walk, I switched on the television to find the Mexican poet Octavio Paz talking about Borges in the past tense. He had died earlier that day, in Geneva.

All that time, of occasional meetings interspersed with long periods of immersion in their texts, gave me a curious and complex connection to both of these men. Rereading them, I see always more clearly the interweaving of their writings and their lives – their poems as incarnations. I find nothing at all contradictory in accommodating them both. Borges used to say that when writers die they become books – a quite satisfactory incarnation in his view. With luck, however, I think they become voices. In many conversations with Borges, from the formal to the fanciful, I realised sharply that to him I existed only as a voice. That may have led to my deep conviction that voice is perhaps the most essential and lasting incarnation of any existence. More than that, it is in voices, far beyond photographs, that the dead continue to live. In the case of Neruda and Borges, their voices were for me the crucial, guiding element in my translating them. I think of their writings as encapsulations of their voices, and I hear them often in my head, always with awe, and with enduring affection.

When the Era Was an Era

Mario Vargas Llosa always provokes attention, for there are few
novelists alive as dedicated as he is to the possibilities of fiction, in
all its moods, modes, and manners. His writing life has been not
just steadily productive but constantly inventive. His novels are so
skillfully put together that they are worth reading simply as literary
constructs, yet he has remained immersed in his own realities, a
writer who wrestles constantly with Latin American contradictions
and ambiguities. He first attracted attention in Spain in 1962, with
the publication of his novel *The Time of the Hero*, the book that is
often credited with bringing the Latin American novelists of his
generation to the world's attention. As a perpetual dissenter, he has
a grave respect for the responsibility of the writer.

La Fiesta del Chivo, which was launched throughout the Spanish-
speaking world by the Spanish publisher Alfaguara, now appears as
The Feast of the Goat, in a fluid and intelligent translation by Edith
Grossman. The Chivo, the Goat of the title, is Rafael Leonidas
Trujillo Molina, who ruled the Dominican Republic with a whim
of iron from 1930 until his assassination in 1961, a time Dominicans
refer to as the Era. Trujillo's power was absolute, his exercise of it
ruthless; he remains in recent memory as one of the waning Latin
American military dictators, some of whom have served as models
for a number of influential Latin American novels – Miguel Angel
Asturias's *El Señor Presidente*, Augusto Roa Bastos's *I, the Supreme*,
Alejo Carpentier's *Reasons of State*, and Gabriel García Márquez's
Autumn of the Patriarch. In the Dominican Republic, there is by
now a vast archive of the Trujillo era ('*Cuando la Era era Era*',
'When the Era *was* an Era', as Dominicans say). The Dominican
historian Bernardo Vega has continued to produce a meticulous
episodic history of the Trujillo years, and numerous memoirs and

fictional versions have appeared in the intervening time. There is no lack of documents, and there have also been substantial studies and biographies of the period. There is, besides, in that small country a considerable residue of vivid human memory, in Dominicans who survived the Era and have saved much of it in anecdotal form.

★

Asked in an interview in the Dominican magazine *La Vida* what led him to write the novel, Vargas Llosa replied as follows:

> 'Well, reading and listening to so many things about Trujillo's times, and about his personality. That happened in 1975, when I spent some months in the Dominican Republic. And then because of that curiosity, that fascination that Trujillo and his times had for me, obviously because he was an emblematic dictator for a slew of authoritarian military regimes that hung over my childhood and my growing up. No question but that when I went to the Dominican Republic in '75, that whole past somehow set off in me a fierce curiosity, and gave me the idea of a novel of that time, but of that time as a lived experience.'

In the Dominican Republic, Trujillo is still a presence, cropping up often in conversation ('*Pero cuando Trujillo . . .*', 'Now in Trujillo's time . . .'), still in the air. I spent a dozen winters in that country, in its most remote province, and I absorbed both its ways and its history, by reading available texts, but more by listening to my neighbors. Most of them neither read nor wrote, but they were nothing if not eloquent. At some distance from a town, we lived by the *chisme*, the local gossip network along which news was passed, most often transformed and domesticated in its passing – my neighbors referred to it as Radio Bemba, 'Radio Lip'.

From these same neighbors, I heard many stories of Trujillo's time, and particularly memories of his two pompous visits to the province. What mostly caught my attention was the habit the men had of lowering their voices whenever they talked about Trujillo. With that more than anything, I felt something of the chill of his continuing presence. The anecdotes were undoubtedly inflated in the imagination and in the telling, but they had an unforgettable mixture of awe and helplessness about them, an overall dread that can never quite be conveyed by facts or texts, but recurs in lived memory.

The Trujillo years were in themselves the stuff of fiction. Externally, they had about them a grandiosity, an obsession with show, with public ostentation. The dictator's megalomania was enshrined in buildings and monuments, in icons and photographs, in public rituals, in his fastidious collection of private uniforms, and in the ubiquitous presence of his name and his shadow. He was a cult in himself, known in turn as the Father of the Country, ultimately as the Benefactor. He was also seen in the popular eye as the great *machista*, the insatiable sexual conqueror of women. The army was his. The Treasury was his. The country was his. Plots and counterplots abounded, but his ruthlessly efficient secret police put a quick end to opposition. As the *campesinos* still say, there was no crime in the pueblos, the price of bread did not rise; but the far reaches of the country were cowed into an awed obedience, a worshipful terror.

★

What is first remarkable about *The Feast of the Goat* is the prodigious amount of work that has gone into the writing – Vargas Llosa spent over three years working on it, and he has made himself familiar with every setting, every atmosphere, every circumstance, every fact in Trujillo's fervid history. None of this absorbed information is wasted; instead, it is stitched invisibly into flashes of memory, conversations, arguments, meditations, all by different characters, throughout the book. The filmic changes of scene that shift the reader's attention are wonderfully managed. The incidents for which Trujillo was most notorious – the abduction and subsequent murder of Jesús de Galíndez, a Basque and a Columbia University instructor, who had written ill of Trujillo, from the New York streets; the horrendous massacre in 1937 of more than 15,000 Haitians, caught on the wrong side of the border, by Dominican troops; the murder of the dissident Mirabal sisters – are all there in variously recollected detail. The novel is, without setting out to be, a startlingly full condensation of the whole Trujillo era, in a welter of lived detail.

Detail, however, does not in any way impede the anxiety of the novel's forward movement. There are three vantage points, three centers of attention, revolving around three sets of characters, and they alternate in our preoccupations over the book's twenty-four chapters. The first is that of the fictional Urania Cabral, a Dominican-born woman in her late forties who works as a lawyer in New York, and has returned to Santo Domingo from an obstinate, self-imposed exile for the first time in thirty-five years to confront her past. The second is that of Trujillo himself, whom the narrative follows through the conversations, confrontations, recollections, and celebrations that make up the working day in 1961 which will end with his assassination. The third is that of the group of conspirators, each with his own distinct motive for wanting to kill Trujillo, waiting in pursuit cars by the Malecón, the seawalk in Santo Domingo, where the dictator's car will pass, they have been assured, later that evening.

These three narrative threads – Urania's painful recovery of her past, Trujillo's machinations with his ministers, advisers, and suppliants throughout one unwinding day, and the unbearable tensions and desperation of the waiting conspirators – all slowly converge in the novel, in melodramatic detail. The book has all the tensions of a doomed adventure, all the murk of plot and conspiracy, of constant fear and ultimate horror.

For the first half of the book, the three threads alternate chapters regularly. But after Trujillo is killed, the assassins' stories take on a dominating momentum: Trujillo's sections stop, Urania's are suspended, and the narrative follows the conspirators as they face the terrible consequences of Trujillo's death. The fear that runs through the book does not disappear with Trujillo's murder; instead it remains in the air and takes a brutal revenge.

★

The book is not simply a recreation of Trujillo, although it does give him a precise and detailed past and a presence full of ruthless self-belief and cruelty but also a secret shame; it is more a demonstration of his utter domination of an entire society, and of the many ambiguous reactions to his absolute power within that society, imprisoned by its own fear, abused, violated, and silenced. What Vargas Llosa has done in *The Feast of the Goat* is to fulfill precisely the intention he expressed in his *La Vida* interview, namely, to recover the time of Trujillo in writing 'as a lived experience'. In that he has been excruciatingly successful; some of his small episodes are hard to bear in their cruelties. They wear the additional horror of having happened.

The pervasive fear of Trujillo that hangs over the events of *The Feast of the Goat*, and the accompanying shame of being humiliated by him, intrude into Urania's memories, into the ponderings of the assassins waiting in the car, and into the dictator's icy confrontations with ministers and supplicants. Trujillo, on the day of his assassination, was dealing with mounting crises in his republic. Because of his brutal record, he had been ostracised by the countries of Latin America and sanctions had been voted against him by the Organisation of American States. His excesses had become an embarrassment to the United States, despite his frequent tactical protestations of anticommunism and his proximity to revolutionary Cuba. He has also been newly defied by the Church, which he had previously taken pains to placate. He has premonitions of an ending, of the fading of his power. But what Trujillo most fears is that he is losing power over his own body – at seventy, the dictator whose fastidiousness and virility are themselves renowned and feared has become incontinent and impotent:

And at that moment, like the blow of a club to his head, he was seized by doubt . . . There it was: the dark stain covered his fly and part of his right leg. It must have been recent, it was still damp, at this very moment his insensible bladder was still leaking. He didn't feel it, he wasn't feeling it. A lashing rage shook him. He could dominate men, bring three million Dominicans to their knees, but he could not control his bladder.

It is the character of Urania Cabral, however, whose return to the Dominican Republic provides the occasion for recalling the events of the past, and it is she who brings the novel to its expiatory ending. A driven lawyer – formerly at the World Bank and now living a successful, solitary life in Manhattan – Urania is deemed coldhearted by both the suitors she rejects and the family in the Dominican Republic whose letters she leaves unanswered. The one link she had allowed herself was reading voraciously about the Trujillo era in her spare time. Now, back in Santo Domingo, where 'her steps, not her will' lead her along the streets to her childhood home, she wonders:

> Were you right to come back? You'll be sorry, Urania. Wasting a week's vacation, when you never had time to visit all the cities, regions, countries you would have liked to see – returning to the island you swore you'd never set foot on again. A symptom of decline? The sentimentality of age? Curiosity, nothing more. To prove to yourself you can walk along the streets of this city that is no longer yours, travel through this foreign country and not have it provoke sadness, nostalgia, hatred, bitterness, rage in you. Or have you come to confront the ruin of your father? To learn what effect seeing him has on you, after so many years?

The scenes in which the bitter, wounded, taunting Urania confronts her father, who has suffered a stroke, strangely echo those of Trujillo wielding power over his underlings. Speaking both aloud to her father and to herself, Urania recreates her childhood, as the only daughter of the widowed Agustín Cabral, one of Trujillo's close advisers, and president of the Senate. Suddenly, he is denounced in the 'Foro Público', the newspaper column Trujillo made use of to indicate changes in his favors.

Deprived of all his posts, facing ruin, Cabral was desperate to recover the dictator's goodwill. Urania was then fourteen, beautiful, intelligent, a favorite of the nuns. A former friend of Cabral's who is still close to Trujillo suggests to Cabral that he might offer his daughter for a private fiesta at the Casa Caoba, Trujillo's country retreat. Urania is coaxed into accepting. Her subsequent rape has changed her life – the nuns manage to send her out of the country, and she has turned her back on it until this return. In the book's last chapter, she recounts the precise events of that evening to her aged aunt, her two muddle-headed cousins, and her young niece. She spares no detail. It is as if she's describing the violation of her entire country. Although Urania begins as an obviously fictional character, a stand-in for the novelist, as she reconnects with place and past, she becomes a crucial decipherer of that past, which has haunted and desexed her. In doing so, she grows increasingly sympathetic to the reader as an inquisitor, a clarifier, and a humanising presence.

★

In April of last year, a few weeks after *La Fiesta del Chivo* appeared in Spanish, Vargas Llosa came to Santo Domingo for the formal *presentación* of his novel. It had been devoured by Dominican readers, and fiercely discussed and reviewed in the press, not always favorably. Some critics searched the text for factual errors, brandishing them like bloodied scalps. Others resented the intrusion of fictional characters like Urania Cabral into a novel that one critic called 'more history than fiction, since the great majority of its characters were real, some of them still living'.

Shortly afterward, the historian Bernardo Vega published a precise list of the thirty-eight errors he discovered in the book, most of them fairly minor – misplaced dates, mistaken affiliations. He quoted García Márquez's remark that for the Latin American writer, the problem is to make the reality credible, for reality is a better writer than they are. While Dominicans talk about the 'Era' among themselves, they are sensitive to the intrusion of outside opinion. In a sense, they have concealed the realities of the Era of Trujillo from themselves, avoiding the shame of having been governed by him. Throughout their long history, the inhabitants of the island have been victimised by intrusions from outside, and they have inherited the psychology of victims. It is their mute complicity with the inflated fictions of the long Trujillo years that still perplexes them, as has Vargas Llosa's unsparing version.

When Vargas Llosa appeared before an audience of some eight hundred people in Santo Domingo last April, he was in his element, poised, lucid, on his own ground, and he made the case for his fiction with an impassioned eloquence. Past events are inevitably altered by the perspectives of time, and by their transformations into language; it was the novelist's function, he felt, to humanise past events as lived experiences, to make a present sense of them. Vargas Llosa showed that evening how thoroughly he has digested

Borges. He is, in Borges's sense, a *ficcionero*, a maker of fictions, which is to say, a maker of meanings. As he writes in his celebrated essay on the subject, 'The Truth of Lies':

> Novels have a beginning and an end and even in the most form-less and intermittent of them, life takes on a meaning that we can perceive because they give us a perspective that real life, in which we are immersed, always denies us. This order is an invention, an addition by the novelist, a simulator who seems to recreate life whereas in truth he is amending it. Sometimes subtly, sometimes brutally, fiction betrays life, encapsulating it in a weft of words which reduces its scale and makes it accessible to the reader. This reader can therefore judge it, understand it, and above all live it, with an impunity that real life does not allow.

He must have been gratified by the intelligent and enthusiastic response of the very audience whose reality he had amended. As we were leaving, a Dominican friend took me aside. 'For us Dominicans,' he said to me, 'this evening was nothing short of an exorcism.'

*

The group of seven conspirators in the novel all have their separate reasons for their desperate venture, their separate shames. Should it succeed, everything would depend on General Roman, the head of the armed forces, who had agreed to initiate a coup on seeing Trujillo's body. Agonisingly, the plot falters, and the conspirators are at once on the run, hunted by the secret police and, except for two who go into protracted hiding, are run down, imprisoned, and tortured. It has always seemed to me that torture is almost an inadmissible territory to writers of fiction, which is to say that it is beyond the imagination. To be made believable, it must have happened. García Márquez has a note on dealing with violence in the novel in volume four of his *Obra Periodistica*, his collected journalism:

> Probably the greatest error of those who have tried to put violence into words has been rather through inexperience or voracity, to

get a hold of leaves rather than the root. Overwhelmed by the available material, they are consumed by the descriptions of massacres, without stopping to ask themselves which matters more in the human and literary sense, the dead, or the living? The exhaustive inventory of decapitations and castrations, of women raped, of genitals and intestines ripped out, and the minute description of the cruelty of these violations, does not lead to fiction. The drama lies more in the pervasive terror brought on by these crimes. The novel arises not from the disemboweled dead but in those still alive, who must in hiding continually feel the icy sweat of fear, knowing that with every heartbeat they run the risk of being themselves disemboweled. Yet those who have confronted such violence and have lived to tell it have not realised that the novel lies not in what happened previously, but rather in the traces of it they feel inside themselves . . .

Vargas Llosa knows this well – his chapters on the flight of the conspirators, with Trujillo dead and the coup failed, are of a chilling intensity. Following their capture, they are subjected to vicious torture. These passages in *The Feast of the Goat* are excruciating to read, yet they have their own authenticity. Because he has been scrupulous about facts, here as elsewhere he gives whatever he touches the authority of the real. For most of his writing life, his preoccupation has been not with human rights so much as with human wrongs. Human rights are abstractions. Human wrongs are more easily recognisable: they are visible and tangible, their measure our shame and our indignation – if the wrongs are our own, shame; if they are the wrongs of others, indignation and horror, as we have been learning of late.

★

Like most of the Latin American writers of his generation, Vargas Llosa has a past of fervent movie-going, and a writing mind that has made full use in novels of the sudden shifts of perspective that can happen so easily on the screen. In novels as crowded with incident as *The Feast of the Goat*, he is in a sense the novelist-as-director. His most admired novel to date, *The War of the End of the*

World, began as a screenplay in the mid-Seventies, and later grew into the majestic novel it became. I translated that screenplay, which was already the blueprint for a much more ambitious piece of writing. The film was never made; the novel usurped it and took its place. While I was reading *La Fiesta del Chivo*, I realised that the novel has already been envisioned as a film, so carefully and precisely placed are its scenes, its flashbacks, its conversations. The cruel theatricality of the Trujillo era almost demands the screen, as Vargas Llosa is well aware. *The Feast of the Goat* is its own screenplay. It deserves to be a terrifyingly good film, for it already is, in written form.

Talking Cuba

'To be Cuban is to be born in Cuba. To be Cuban is to go with Cuba everywhere. To be Cuban is to carry Cuba like a persistent memory. We all carry Cuba within like an unheard music, like a rare vision that we know by heart. Cuba is a paradise from which we flee by trying to return.'

In *Mea Cuba*, Guillermo Cabrera Infante gathers together all the separate writings on Cuba – articles, essays, memoirs, portraits, reflections, prepared talks – that he has produced since October 3, 1965, the day he left Cuba on a flight to Belgium (where he had been serving as cultural attaché) on the understanding of the authorities that he would not return for two years. His own understanding was different. As the plane passed the point of no return, he says,

I knew then what would be my destiny: to travel without returning to Cuba, to care for my daughters and to occupy myself by/in literature. I don't know whether or not I pronounced the magic formula – 'silence, exile, cunning' – but I can say that it is easier in this time to adopt the literary style than to copy the lifestyle of James Joyce.

Cabrera Infante's exile has lasted just short of thirty years by now, in the course of which he has become an enduringly original literary presence, unquestionably Cuba's most important living writer, and one who, more than the other Latin American writers of his generation, has intruded himself into the English language, writing occasionally in an English as startling and original as his Spanish, and masterminding the translations of his own work into English.

Inevitably, since *Mea Cuba* is as personal as its title suggests, its underlying theme, its underlying reality, is that of exile. When

Cabrera Infante left Cuba, he first came to rest in Spain, but, denied permanent residence there, he moved to London, where he has lived steadily since 1966, in about as un-Cuban a setting as can be imagined. In an interview he gave a few years ago, he said: 'I inhabit three islands: the British Isles, of which I am now a citizen; Cuba, which is always in my being and my memory, and the top of my desk, which is my active, everyday island.' Most tellingly, however, exile for him meant exile from his language, not just Spanish, but Cuban Spanish, with its quickness of tongue, wryly admired in Spanish America. In the short memoir, 'Two Died Together', in *Mea Cuba*, Cabrera Infante writes of Cubans talking:

> A *tasca* in old Madrid on a November afternoon in 1976. Two middle-aged men are talking seated at a table. One of them is an imposing black who could easily play Othello, the other is white, short, with protruding eyes that seem to see everything. He could be played by Peter Lorre in *Casablanca*. Both are Cuban, both exiles and they have been talking louder than the Madrileños around them – and that's saying a lot . . . They are, from right to left, Gastón Baquero and Enrique Labrador Ruiz. They are talking their way downhill. When there is a clearing in their conversation, one hears an unusual thunder: the whole *tasca* applauds. They are still applauding the two Cubans who talked. They heard them as one hears rain at first, then they listened attentively, then they applauded deafeningly. The Madrileños, who know about *tasca* talk, recognised the two foreigners for what they were: masters of conversation . . . The two friends in the *tasca* were both exiles and the only thing left to them in life was their art. In which figured, prominently, conversation.

There are many parallels between his situation and that of Vladimir Nabokov – it was in his writing, too, that Cabrera Infante could recover and keep alive the country he had left, with no prospect of returning. Without choosing, he had become, to himself, an outpost of the Cuban language in London, something like a literary embassy, without portfolio. As a consequence, language became his reality. Language, insofar as he could keep it alive, was all he had of Cuba, all that he could take with him.

★

Born in 1929, three years younger than Fidel Castro, Cabrera Infante, whose parents were founding members of the Cuban Communist Party, came of age with the Revolution. In *Mea Cuba*, in the long essay 'Bites from the Bearded Crocodile', on the effect of the Revolution on Cuban writers, he recalls its first days:

> When Fidel Castro entered Havana in January 1959 like a larger Christ (as Severo Sarduy wrote from Paris with love), some of us saw him as some kind of younger, bearded version of Magwitch: a tall outlaw emerging from the fog of history to make political Pips of us all. However, the outlaw never became an in-law, only a law unto himself: the Redeemer was always wearing a gun on his hip.

Almost immediately Cabrera Infante was appointed editor of *Lunes de Revolución*, the literary supplement of the newspaper *Revolución* that served as the main voice of the new government. As editor, he gave the necessary support to his brother Saba to complete a short documentary film, *P.M.,* an excursion into the night life in the bars and clubs of Havana at the time. Submitted to the official censorship, the film was accused of being counter-revolutionary, and banned. Outraged, Cabrera Infante used *Lunes* to protest, and brought down on his head something of a show trial, at which Fidel Castro himself addressed the assembled intellectuals on their duties to the Revolution. Soon afterward, *Lunes* was closed down, and Cabrera Infante found himself in the kind of limbo many Cuban writers of his generation were to inhabit in succeeding years, forbidden to publish. 'Within the Revolution, everything! Against the Revolution, nothing!' as Fidel 'thundered like a thousand Zeuses'. It was the fate that was to overtake the poet Heberto Padilla in 1971, when he was forced to make a ludicrous public confession of the anti-revolutionary bent of his writing. His case caused many writers throughout Latin America to break openly with the cause of Cuba.

Cabrera Infante was sent to Brussels as cultural attaché; but when he returned to Cuba in 1965 to attend his mother's funeral, he was made to realise the precariousness of any continuing Cuban existence under an imposed silence, and he accepted the inevitability of exile. The greatest deprivation of exile for Cabrera Infante turned out to be his isolation from the living, shifting language of everyday Havana; but that very circumstance did much to form his prose from that time on. The work-in-progress he carried with him when he left Cuba, the book later published as *Tres tristes tigres* in 1967, was written almost exclusively in a spoken language, spoken Cuban.

Cabrera Infante has resisted calling it a novel. It is a vast linguistic flight through the nightlife and night-happenings of a group of young Cubans, as meticulously set in a real Havana as was Joyce's *Ulysses* in Dublin, a spontaneous native Havana-by-night that would soon be forced underground. Its antecedents are the *Satyricon* of Petronius and the Night-town chapter of *Ulysses*. The events, encounters, characters, conversations, arguments, and musings of five Cubans pass through all manner of linguistic modes, and the characters play throughout with many forms of public language – literature, advertising, popular song, local legend, propaganda, the movies, the comics. The spoken language, with its jokes, puns, antic quotations, and irreverent parody, is also playing with the dire realities behind it – the point is that in the spoken language alone the characters are alive and have their being. Living speech free to run wild, is life-giving; the pathos lies in the inevitable return at the night's end to silence.

It had been Cabrera Infante's intention when he began the book to offset the passages of nighttime extravagance and excess with scenes from Cuba's new daytime reality, the revolutionary zeal that ran directly counter to the irreverences of the night: he would thus suggest the contradictions he lived through as a writer in Cuba. Once in exile, however, he saw that the life of his book lay in the spoken nighttime exuberances of his characters, although the Revolution is everpresent as backdrop and circumstance; and he finished the book accordingly. None of the very substantial novels that were being published in Latin America at the time came anything close to its originality and verbal agility; and few works in Spanish are as hilariously and irreverently funny. It is literature as performance – it can be read on different levels of attention, although language itself is its constant subject-matter. It is also a book to be heard as well as read.

Tres tristes tigres is Cabrera Infante's seminal work, and it greatly helped to set for Cabrera Infante the mode and manner of the writing that was to follow, as he faced the blank silence of exile. In many passages like this one from *Tres tristes tigres*, the Revolution intrudes into reverie:

> He made a muffled sound. What does a sound look like in its muffler? Idiocy of the folk. Muffled noises. Empty vessels make muffled sounds. Sounds to all deaf. Deaf words falling on silk purposes. Till deaf do us part. The early bird catches the first post. You can lead a horse to the water but you can't make him think. (Though you can make him sink.) Too many cocks spoil the brothel. We need a revolution among proverbs, for God's sake. Proverbs a la lanterne. Anyone who says a proverb should be shot. Ten sayings that shook the workers. Marx, Marx-Mao, Mao-Mao. It's a Mao's world. Soldiers, from the height of this sentence twenty centuries and Big Brother are watching you. Wiscondom of the folk. A phantom is hunting Europe, it is the phantom of Stalin. Crime, how many liberties have been taken in thy name. One must tend socialist man, as one would tend a tree. Ready. Aim. Timmmmmbeeerrrr! A call of duty is a beast forever. Isn't it true? Isn't it true? Isn't it? True.

The sheer fact that spoken language shifts constantly, makes sudden connections, plays with itself, asks and answers with a rapidity and an immediacy that a written language is at slow pains to match led Cabrera Infante to write from that point on deliberately in a spoken language, a language of sheer nerve, one that was free to play, to pun, to make spontaneous connections, to tease a subject, to go at times where language led, to perform a written language that at every point drew attention to itself as language, deceptive and unreliable as it might be clarifying. As a writer, he chose to become a speaking voice, varying between the reportorial and the wry, as here, in an essay called 'Actors and Sinners':

Fidel Castro is perhaps the best television actor in the world, with a mastery of the medium and an absolute control not only of his voice and his gestures but of his temper. I remember having seen him one day in the waiting room of a television studio about to go on the air. Meanwhile, he killed time joking, strolling around calmly as he slowly smoked his habitual Havana, talking about cows and green pasturage and milk production, smiling satisfied: the agreeable agronomist. But no sooner had they introduced him to the well-lit studio and the camera had focused on him, than he came on the air transformed into a true Zeus thundering terrible traumas against an invisible opposition. He was not the elder Marx but the young Jupiter.

At the same time, however, Cabrera Infante was living in English, entering the language, writing (in English) the screenplay for the film *Vanishing Point*, and supervising the enormous task of turning the untranslatable flights of *Tres tristes tigres* into English, becoming in fact a bilingual being. As happened in Nabokov's case, exile had the effect of intensifying and heightening language for him, and the books he wrote from now on were all destined to have an English existence, masterminded by him. He wore both languages easily, and they cross-fertilised each other. In England especially, his command of the language has brought him both respect and attention.

In 1981, he published in the *London Review of Books* his long essay on Cuban writers, 'Bites from the Bearded Crocodile', his first deliberate writing in English (he had later to translate it for the Spanish edition of *Mea Cuba*, as he did the hilarious memoir, *Holy Smoke*, which he wrote soon after in English). He did not, however, follow Conrad and Nabokov in becoming an English writer, although he was already wittily present as one. Cuba was still what he was composed of, and he determinedly remained a 'writer of Cuban'. All his work, consequently, skirts on autobiography, but while it feeds freely on past realities, it also sends them up, burlesquing them, peering at them from new and startling sides. In *Infante's Inferno*, the picaresque erotic memoir he wrote of his earlier years in Havana, puns abound, ever more energetically, each one a tugging reminder that we are at the mercy of language and the surprise turns it takes.

Mea Cuba gathers together pieces written irregularly over twenty-four years, close to seventy in all, some of them long, free-ranging essays, some of them short and pithy retorts to critics, some of them written addresses, some of them short reflections. The cast of characters is vast and recurring – friends and colleagues dead or exiled or silent, or caught up in the mechanism of the Revolution. Since Cabrera Infante was bent on preserving his Havana in writing, the detail is sharp, although the ironies are never far away, the tone increasingly sardonic as the book progresses. As opposed to its gleeful predecessors, *Mea Cuba* is in a sense a reluctant book, one that he would hardly have chosen to write had it not more or less accrued through time.

When he first settled in England, Cabrera Infante kept silent on matters Cuban for some time (silence, exile, cunning). In August of 1968 he was officially expelled from the Union of Writers and Artists of Cuba, as a traitor to the revolutionary cause, and he simultaneously broke his silence on Cuba, in articles and interviews in the press, in Spain and Latin America, and also in occasional lectures. He asks in his preface.

> What's a man like me doing in a book like this? Nobody considers me a political writer nor do I consider myself a politician. But it happens that there are occasions when politics is intensely transformed into an ethical activity.

The voice throughout these pieces is an essentially ethical one, withering and sardonic in its denouncing of human wrongs, bitter in its ironies, fierce in its dismissals. At the same time, however, he chronicles his time and situation in Cuba with enlivening recall, and peoples it with the lost friends and enemies who defined him then, particularly the writers who inevitably found themselves in the same stifling position that had forced him into exile, wondering whether anyone in Cuba would see their work. In an address he delivered in Madrid in 1990, reprinted in *Mea Cuba*, Cabrera Infante makes the observation:

According to an English writer who visited Havana last year my books were the object of a strange cult among the ruins. Smuggled into the country, they were sold under the counter for the price of – ten tins of condensed milk! *La Habana Para un Infante Difunto* was then on the list of the best milked books. In the first slot, uncomfortably placed, was a book about perestroika (which in Havana is pronounced '*la espera estoica*' – the stoic wait), its author called, he is still called, Mikhail Gorbachev. It was the first time that in Communist Cuba a Soviet author collected his officially tax-exempt royalties not in pesos but in barter.

Asides on the ambiguous state of exile are threaded throughout the book.

Cuba is the country that has produced the most exiles during more than a century and a half of American history . . . for us Cubans this is the century of exile . . . A million and a half Cubans have already taken the landless road.

Such a diaspora has made inevitable an outpouring of writing on Cuba over the last thirty years, a whole literature of frustration. It seems to me that Cabrera Infante stands quite obstinately apart from that writing, in his stoical acceptance of 'the violation of geography by history', and in his sardonic independence of mind and manner. It is the island of his desk that is his true territory. His fierce exercise of his freedom to write more than compensates for the pain of exile, and the accompanying running guilt at being 'here rather than there'.

Most of the essays in *Mea Cuba* re-create the characters and lived circumstances during the years of descending limbo in Cuba, between 1959 and 1965, and the two people who figure most prominently in these chronicles are José Lezama Lima, the poet of Gongoresque density who was acknowledged as master of Cuban letters at the time of the Revolution, and Virgilio Piñera, the Cuban playwright, both of who served as mentors to Cabrera Infante. Both were homosexual; neither of them was at all adept at reading the changing political climate of the Revolution. They were doomed to be its victims, driven to a kind of internal emigration, to an enforced silence.

Cabrera Infante's re-creation of them, affectionate in detail and abundant in anecdote, dramatises painfully and compassionately their inevitable suffocation. When the hearings against *Lunes* were being held, attended by Castro himself, Lezama Lima, who had himself been attacked in *Lunes*, nevertheless made a speech invoking the eternity of art and the permanence of culture. This was a characteristic imprudence, since Castro followed by denouncing all cultural divergence in the name of art (which applied even to long hair), by excoriating homosexuals in particular, and eventually persecuting them actively. Anything at all that smacked of the 'degenerate' Cuba of Batista, any vestige of the nightworld Cuba Cabrera Infante was at such pains to document and preserve in *Tres tristes tigres*, had to be obliterated, cleansed, rehabilitated by the Revolution, and writers and artists, dangerously unreliable in such a light, had no choice but to surrender their lives, in one sense or the other.

Since this realisation set clearly and implacably in Cabrera Infante's mind, his position on Cuba has never wavered. Cuba has been since the Sixties a tyranny, the Revolution long since perverted and betrayed. Illusions about the regime and justifications for it are to be revealed and exploded. He has also kept strenuously clear of the factionalism of Cuban exiles. His own stern and sardonic eye has been enough for him. Literature, the act of writing, has been for him life-giving, life-sustaining.

Cabrera Infante's writings stand out sharply from other writings on Cuba from the outside. They are fiercely personal and they have no particular case to make, no cause to argue. The numerous lives they summon up are anything but case studies – they are real people, rounded out and intricately remembered. Scorn there is in abundance, most of the rampant ridicule reserved for Fidel Castro, whom Cabrera Infante knew and observed in adolescence. In *Mea Cuba*, he is mostly referred to, for simplicity's sake, as The Tyrant. He is variously to Cabrera Infante a figure become prehistoric by now, an actor who has totally consumed the stage, but who has survived in power only through creating a web of informers so vast as to sow distrust into the texture of everyday life in Cuba. In a long review-essay on Robert E. Quirk's biography of Fidel Castro,

Cabrera Infante writes:

> Nevertheless Fidel Castro went on swamping the land with slogans concocted by this Maximum Publicist. See some samples: 'Join the War Against All Weeds', 'Land or Death!' To bigger billboards urging all Cubans to the joys of 'Artificial Insemination – Not One Cow Left Barren!' It was a campaign that lasted two generations of Cubans. Not two years ago he exhorted all good men and true to do battle for the potato. 'This is a battle we must win,' he said on the May Day parade. 'We will win the battle for the potato.' It was more Groucho than Karl: 'Potatoes of the country, unite! You have nothing to lose but your roots!' Potatory.

One of the studies in the book that show Cabrera Infante at his very best as a chronicler is his account of the life and times of Capablanca, the Cuban chess master, which begins with a three-year-old Cabrera Infante being taken by his mother to see the catafalque of the Great Cuban. The unwinding of Capablanca's character, career, and chess prowess through anecdote and aside, the range of reference and analogy Cabrera Infante sneaks into the text, the relish in the prose, give the whole essay the quality and completeness of a film.

> *Could Fischer have defeated Capablanca?* Fischer sought always to demolish his opponent, physically and mentally. The only way that Fischer would have been able to finish off Capablanca would have been to take advantage when Capa pressed the button of his timer to have, behind Fischer's back, a parade of chorus-girls, models and stripteasers to distract the naked eye of the Cuban.

There is a richly funny essay, 'Actors and Sinners', on politicians-as-actors-as -politicians. There is also a moving essay of farewell to Néstor Almendros, the Spanish cinematographer who had become an 'honorary Cuban' in Cabrera Infante's eyes, and who remained a constant friend in all Cabrera Infante's close ties with cinema. The pieces in *Mea Cuba* can so often shift in mood, go grave or antic by stages, turn a subject on its ear, reduce a gravity to absurdity, that the reader has to remain on his toes.

Whatever the deprivations and invisibilities of exile, and quite apart from the remarkable literature he has produced, Cabrera Infante has by now earned for himself an unusual position, that of a small and ferociously independent outclave of Cuba, something of a conscience to Cubans, particularly those in exile. His view of Cuba is as clear as it is relentless, and he has Cuba at heart. His writings reveal that he is a Cuban to be trusted. It is not every Cuba-in-the-making these days that will be able to look a book like *Mea Cuba* in the eye.

'After scientific analysis only prophecy, it seems to me, is left,' he writes in the essay 'And of My Cuba, What?'

When tyrannies succumb they leave behind the enormous weight of the past and no visible, foreseeable future – only the present can be creative. Thus one will have to extend the present of all Cubans to the immediate future, tomorrow, to wonder, and of my Cuba, what? To hear the echo that answers as if a sonorous mirror, '*What Cuba?*'

Troublemaker

Among the Latin American writers who have attracted attention since the Sixties, Reinaldo Arenas has remained somewhat on the periphery, even although his books have been translated in many languages and, certainly in Europe, enthusiastically received. A great deal of this has to do with his being Cuban. Born in 1943, he came of age with the revolution, and, given the extraordinary gift he demonstrated with his first book, he might conceivably have become a star of the new Cuba. But rebellion against unjust authority came naturally to him, and his life in Cuba was one of increasing trouble. His open homosexuality marked him as a victim, and the fact that the novels that brought him acclaim in Spain and France had been smuggled out of Cuba without official permission led to his being kept under constant surveillance and then, in 1970, imprisoned. A few years after he was released he escaped in the Mariel boatlift in 1980.

His books are demanding. The five novels of his *pentagonía*, the recreation of his Cuba, are not novels in any conventional sense. In them, separate stories crowd in on one another, hallucinatory passages give way to disembodied conversation, in the first person and in the third person. There are long passages of pure lyrical writing in which the distinction between poetry and prose is blurred. Meditations are sometimes juxtaposed with official documents – reality is multifaceted, contradictory, labyrinthine. Yet throughout, the books show a high literary intelligence and a voluptuous command of different modes of language, from hallucinatory flight to science fiction. Also, his books appeared in irregular order in other countries, while he remained in Cuba, out of reach. After he died at the end of 1990 he left behind for his readers, in the form of a memoir, a map of the reality from which they were made, *Before Night Falls*.

He completed the memoir in New York City in August of 1990, scarcely four months before he took his own life. To complete it was part of the plan he set himself three years previously, when he was diagnosed as having AIDS. He describes how, on his return from hospital in 1987:

> I dragged myself toward a photograph I have on my wall of Virgilio Piñera the older Cuban writer, whom he particularly respected as an 'incessant rebel', and who died in Havana before he left and I spoke to him in this way:
>
> 'Listen to what I have to tell you: I need three more years of life to finish my work, which is my vengeance against most of the human race.'
>
> I think Virgilio's face darkened, as if I had asked for something outrageous. It is almost three years now since that desperate request. My end is near. I expect to keep myself calm and collected until the very end.
>
> Thank you, Virgilio.

In spite of various stays in hospital, he turned these three years to furious account. He completed the writing of *The Color of Summer*, the remaining volume of his *pentagonía*, the spine of his written work, and he revised the unpublished text of his novel *The Assault*. He put in order other texts that are still to be published, and went over the translation of *The Doorman*, the most lightheartedly inventive of his novels, a fable of the pains of exile, written in New York. He visited his friend Jorge Camacho in Spain and with him, in the fall of 1988, he issued an open letter to Fidel Castro asking for free elections in Cuba, a letter that was signed by other writers and widely published later that year. And he wrote *Before Night Falls*, a terse and detailed accounting of his life, particularly about his treatment by the Cuban regime, dictating the entire book, and then correcting the transcript. As he worked, he was well aware that these were to be his last words.

*

Before Night Falls is an extraordinary book, extraordinary in its restraint and its dignity, particularly in view of the tribulations that seemed always to dog him. He had every reason in the world to write his book of 'vengeance against most of the human race', as he promised the photograph of Virgilio Piñera; yet the tone of the book, while not without its sardonic asides, is calm, dispassionate, spare. It makes no argument; instead it recreates a life that, so passionately lived and so desperate to find space for itself, is beyond argument. The face of Reinaldo Arenas that fixes the reader from the book jacket has a gaze, wary and relentless at once, that has to be met. It is the face of an Ancient Mariner, come to tell his tale.

In New York in 1980 Arenas wrote:

> To write, or create, is an act of irreverence, as much ethically as stylistically . . . The novelist, perhaps more than any other kind of author, needs both space and time, spiritually as much as materially, to be able to conceive and realise his work.

What is most affecting about his memoir is Arenas's account of his fierce struggle to secure that minimal freedom, his insistent search for that very space and time to write in a Cuba that increasingly denied it to him. He claimed the same freedom for himself sexually, to a point of recklessness. Of Havana in the 1960s and 1970s he writes: 'I think that the sexual revolution in Cuba actually came about as a result of the existing sexual repression. Perhaps as a protest against the regime, homosexuality began to flourish with ever-increasing defiance.' To be an active homosexual was to choose a way of life fraught with danger, for many of his former friends and lovers turned informer, and homosexuals were increasingly persecuted by the revolution; many of them were sent to forced labor in the cane fields or to concentration camps. Arenas, as both an open homosexual and a dissident writer, was doubly doomed; the circle of his freedom was shrinking all the time.

*

Readers of Arenas's novels will find in *Before Night Falls* the sources of many of his stories and the events in them; what they will not find, however, is their stylistic brilliance, their flights of language. The language of the memoir is stark, the sentences short and staccato, with an urgency of forward movement. He is recalling his life, ticking it off in sharp, remembered moments, against the clock, with death waiting at his elbow. He recalls his childhood in a series of short icon-like chapters, a childhood that he recreated in rhapsodic fullness in his first novel, *Celestino antes del alba* (*Singing from the Well*). His father was an 'adventurer' who left his mother before he was born. He grew up in a houseful of women without men, presided over by his grandmother, in a poor country district in Oriente, in the obliterative poverty of Batista's declining dictatorship. He describes the peasant superstitition by which 'my grandmother would try to drive away hurricanes by making crosses with ashes', and the violent natural life of the countryside:

At night we could hear the screeches of the frogs as they were slowly swallowed by small snakes; you could hear the squeak of a mouse being torn to pieces by a gnome owl; the desperate cackle of a hen being throttled and swallowed by a Cuban boa; the kicking and muffled cry of a rabbit quartered in the air by an owl, or the bleating sheep cut to pieces by wild dogs. The noise, the desperate clamors, the dull stamping, all those sounds were familiar companions . . .

At one point he writes, 'I think that splendor of my childhood was unique because it was absolute poverty but also absolute freedom; out in the open, surrounded by trees, animals, apparitions, and people who were indifferent toward me. My existence was not even justified, nobody cared.' That insistence on freedom became the single driving force of his existence, as his writing became its outward manifestation. It is to those years too that he surely owed his stoical determination to survive.

Hunger drove him in 1958, at the age of fifteen, to join the rebels in the Gibara mountains. Although he did not take part in the fighting, he joined in the general euphoria at Batista's sudden collapse. As he says: 'In those days I was part of the Revolution; I had nothing to lose, and it seemed then that I had much to gain.' What he did gain was a scholarship to study agricultural accounting, coupled with indoctrination, followed by work on a chicken farm in Oriente, and eventually a course in economic planning at the

University of Havana. The move to Havana was a move from the solitude that had cloaked him to a world of encounters and erotic adventure. It also coincided with his emerging as a writer. By chance, he entered a story-telling competition at the National Library, and as a consequence was given a post there that allowed him to disentangle himself from agricultural accounting and devote himself almost entirely to reading and writing, hungry as he was for both.

★

There he wrote *Celestino antes del alba*, and he submitted it in 1965 to a competition sponsored by the Cuban Writers and Artists Union (UNEAC). It won him an award; and when the following year his second novel, *Elmundo alucinante*, gained an honorable mention, his originality as a writer had to be taken into account. He was, after all, of the generation that was expected to produce a novelist of the revolution, and the revolution needed its writers. More importantly for him, this success brought him the friendship of José Lezama Lima and Virgilio Piñera, both homosexuals, both in disfavor with the revolution in spite of their considerable reputations. They became his literary mentors, at a time when he needed them, and he was sustained by their friendship when friendship had become a doubtful quantity.

Celestino was published in Havana in 1967, in a small edition (it was the only one of Arenas's books ever to be published in Cuba). One day, Arenas received a call at the National Library from a Cuban painter called Jorge Camacho, who was visiting from Paris and who had read Arenas's novel. Camacho and his wife, Margarita, formed a strong friendship with Arenas, which was to be a sustaining force throughout his time in Cuba. On their return to Paris, they carried with them his first two novels, which were immediately contracted for and published in Spain and France to considerable critical success. Paradoxically, this further aggravated his situation; when his second novel appeared in French in 1969, it shared the award given in Paris for Best Foreign Novel with García Márquez's *One Hundred Years of Solitude*. He had not, however, sought the authorisation of UNEAC, but had smuggled his manuscripts out of the country. From this point on, the terms of his existence changed drastically. He was put under surveillance by State Security, and went from struggling to become a writer to struggling to survive as one.

In March of 1968, a chapter from his first novel was published in *Mundo Nuevo*, the magazine Emir Rodríguez Monegal edited in Paris which set in motion the boom in Latin American writing. Arenas was then forced by UNEAC to write an open letter to Rodríguez Monegal repudiating the publication and denouncing the review as 'an organ of the CIA for corrupting the intellectuals of Latin America'. At the same time, he smuggled out, through the connections the Camachos always managed to keep open, an appreciative letter to Monegal, explaining the circumstances in which he had been told he had to write the official letter.

For Arenas, the connection to the Camachos was vital, for it was through them that his manuscripts could reach the outside, be published, and so confirm his existence. Of them, he writes in *Before Night Falls*:

> For more than twenty years, one way or another, they have always managed to keep in touch with me, through a passing tourist, a coded message in a letter mailed via the usual channels, a postcard, a notice of an exhibit, a book, and hundreds of little attentions that helped to keep me going during the almost fifteen years I remained in Cuba after our first meeting.

Their constant care and concern for Arenas were heroic; that link kept him alive.

From 1970 on, when the revolution took its Stalinist turn, Arenas was seen by the regime as a man to be punished. He was first sent for six months to a labor camp in Pinar del Río, where he was ostracised and forbidden to write or to publish anything. The official humiliation of the poet Heberto Padilla in 1971, forced publicly to confess along with other Cuban writers to crimes against the revolution, led many intellectuals previously sympathetic to the revolution to denounce it openly. Soon after, Castro defiantly convened his First Congress of Education and Culture, which made it clear that there was no room in Cuba for cultural divergence in the name of art, and which went out of its way to excoriate homosexuals.

★

At this point, the memoir seems to change gear, to quicken. Freedom for Arenas now exists only as a private act, secret and dangerous, and yet he remains defiantly, recklessly free in his many sexual encounters, in outwitting the authorities, in his constant search for a safe shelter, and in the increasingly difficult business of concealing his manuscripts from the police. Every encroachment by the authorities seems to generate a fierce counteractivity on his part, an unpremeditated defiance. In 1969, when he had finished the manuscript of *Otra Vez el Mar*, the third novel of his *pentagonía*, he hid the manuscript with a friend, who transferred it in a moment of panic into the care of two old ladies who lived at the beach. They read some of the book and, very devout, were horrified by its content. Whether they destroyed it or not, it never reappeared. He writes: 'One day at the beach, thinking of my lost book, feeling as if I had lost one of my children, the most beloved, I realised, all of a sudden, that I had to go back home to my typewriter and start again. There was no other way.'

Two years later, he had rewritten the novel. This manuscript he hid under the roof tiles of his aunt's house. When, newly released from prison, he went to recover it, it was gone; and he was made aware that it was in the hands of State Security, where he did not dare to reclaim it. So, begging the use of a typewriter, he wrote it a third time, this time managing to smuggle the manuscript out of the country. In view of the lyrical density of that novel, and the intricacy of its structure, it seems astonishing that he could carry it entire in his head. Yet one feels at once in all his novels the presence of an inestimable writer whose language seemed to flood out of him.

The years between 1973 and 1980 turned to nightmare. He was arrested and accused of being a 'homosexual and enemy of the Revolution'. He escaped, was recaptured and sent to El Morro prison, where he remained until 1976. His account in the memoir of the horrors of prison and his interrogation by State Security has a kind of documentary matter-of-factness that takes hold of the reader.

The most dangerous criminals and the prisoners who ranked as ward 'chiefs' would steal everything. Sometimes you had to go to mess hall carrying your few possessions – a piece of bread, a little bit of sugar, even your pillow. I did not let go of my *Iliad*, which I knew was much coveted by other prisoners, not for its literary value but because with its fine paper they could roll 'cigarettes' by using the stuffing of bunk mattresses or pillows. Books were in great demand; prisoners used them as toilet paper, in those toilets full of shit and flies that fed on the shit, and then buzzed around us all the time. My ward was near the toilet and I had to bear not only the stench but also the noise of the bowel movements. Sometimes a special kind of herb was used in the food, on purpose I think, to cause diarrheoa among the prisoners; it was horrible to have to listen from my bunk, surrounded by flies, to those furious discharges, those incessant farts, excrement falling on excrement, right next to my ward. Our bodies were so impregnated with the stench that it became part of us.

Taking a bath was something almost theoretical. Every other week, on visiting days, the ward chiefs would fill some tanks with water and we would have to line up naked and walk by those tanks, where the chiefs would fill a jug with water and pour it over each of us. We would continue to walk, soaping up until we again passed by the chiefs, who would throw another jug of water at us. But even that sort of bath was a great comfort to us. The ward chiefs would stand on top of the tanks, sticks in hand, and if anyone tried to take a second bath, they would beat him up.

Needless to say, within that group of men there were some queers who would check out the young men with good physiques and proposition them later; there was also an occasional faggot who had managed to be there with his lover. At the baths I once saw all the ward chiefs fucking an adolescent who was not even gay. One day the boy asked to be transferred out. He spoke with one of the guards and explained his predicament, but the soldier ignored him, so he had to keep on making his ass available, against his will, to all those people. Moreover, he had to wash all their clothes, take care of their things, and give them part of the food allotted to him. Like slaves, the poor fairies and defenseless adolescents had to shoo away the flies and fan those criminals.

As for himself he writes, 'I had no sexual relations while in prison, not only as a precaution but because it made no sense; love has to be free, and prison is a monstrosity where love turns into bestiality.' Cornered by State Security, kept under interrogation for four months, he was forced to write and sign a confession. 'After the confession I had nothing; I had lost my dignity and my rebellious spirit . . . Moreover, after my confession they could also obliterate me physically.'

He had no life left in Cuba. Because of the attention drawn to his case by the Camachos in France, because of the following his books had gained outside Cuba, State Security did not dare let him leave the island; free, he was a danger to them. On his side, to continue to write and send out his work would doom him. All he could think of was escape. He had not, however, lost his rebellious spirit as he feared – there is a kind of quiet glee in his account of further evasions, further survivals, as there is in the story of his escape. A savage humor is never very far away. When the authorities guaranteed exit permits to 'antisocials' who wished to leave the island, following the mass occupation of the grounds of the Peruvian Embassy in April 1980, Arenas applied for an exit permit from local authorities, who did not check with State Security; he was lucky to avoid their scrutiny. He arrived in Florida just short of his thirty-seventh birthday.

*

Arenas had left Cuba, but it had not left him. Now, in exile, he had physical freedom, but he no longer possessed the reality that had engaged him; he felt himself a ghost. In the United States, besides, he was to discover that there were many, not all of them Cuban, who carried different Cubas in their heads. From Miami, 'which was like a caricature of Cuba, the worst of Cuba', he fled to

New York. At least he had, as he said at the time, the freedom 'to scream'. With a group of others who had arrived by way of Mariel, he started a magazine; he continued to work on the remaining books of his *pentagonía*; he published, in Mexico in 1986, a book of essays and letters called *Necesidad de Libertad*, which vented all his rages, all his griefs. He lectured, he traveled. In 1983, for the first time since 1967, he was reunited with the Camachos in Spain. And he contracted AIDS.

'Most people are unable to understand us nor should we expect them to; they have their own terrors, and, even if they wanted to, cannot really fathom ours, much less share them.' So writes Arenas of his exile, with Cuban Americans as much in mind as New Yorkers. Inasmuch as he always refused to be a pawn in other people's games, his memoir by its nature remains a purely personal accounting, not a weapon for the use of others. If anyone was entitled to his rage, it was Arenas. *Before Night Falls* might well have been a long cry of anger, a diatribe, but it is marked much more by its fierce determination to describe his experience honestly and incontrovertibly than by anger or self-pity.

There can be a vast distance between those who proclaim human rights and those who return, like the Ancient Mariner, with their tales and evidence of human wrongs. A bent for writing like that of Arenas would have been recognised in many other countries and given ample room in which to develop; but since he was never given any room he could count on, his enormous energy was compressed to an explosive degree. He was forced into defiance, into attitudes and actions he would never have chosen. He claimed, after all, to be no more than a writer and a chronicler: his cause was his own. Like most writers, all he wanted was to see his books published; they were his justification. He ends the memoir with a luminous meditation on being freed from the past, with death waiting. 'Now, the state of grace that had saved me from so many misfortunes had come to an end.' There is a noble and imperturbable dignity about *Before Night Falls*; it is a book above all about being free.

ON TRANSLATION

In writing an original poem, we are translating the word, transmuting it. Everything we do is translation, and all translations are in a way creations.

Octavio Paz

I had never given a thought to translation until I began to read, extensively, poetry in Spanish, and occasionally to tinker with poems I felt in tune with, to see if they could survive in an English version, given Robert Frost's notorious pronouncement that poetry is 'what gets lost in translation'. Translation is a mysterious alchemy; and although the sound patterns of the original poem can never be precisely reproduced, poems have an essence that hovers above and beyond language, and which, with luck, can be kept alive.

A. R.

La Mutualidad: Translation as a Pleasure

When I look back on the whole business of translating, now that I have left it behind (except in the case of occasional enthusiasms), I realise that it has much in common with solitary confinement, the translator shuttered up with a text, dictionaries and blank paper, sentenced to producing an acceptable version that will free him. Nor do translations yield up anything like the satisfaction of writing: I have found it to be dangerous to pick them up, once published, for they are never perfect, and inevitably I begin to tinker with them all over again, for translating is something of an addiction. I think I have kicked the habit, but, as with cigarettes, one can never be sure.

I had a few translating experiences, however, that I remember with sheer pleasure, and I feel it worthwhile to describe them, for they might save embryo translators from some of the pains of solitude. The most consistent pleasure I had came from working with Heberto Padilla. I had first known his poems while he was still in Cuba, under house arrest. Some of his new poems filtered out, and I translated them, out of admiration, for the *New York Review of Books*, which had a lot to do with Padilla's eventual release. When he was free to come to New York, in 1980, we met, became friends, and began to work together. I undertook to translate Heberto's *Selected Poems*, but chose to do them in conjunction with another translator, Andrew Hurley, for I was not eager for more enforced solitude. I had also come to appreciate the value of more than one ear, more than one eye. I talked over some of the more complicated poems with Heberto, and then went for the winter to Puerto Rico, where Hurley lives, in the course of which we prepared our first versions of the poems. At one point, Padilla turned up in Puerto Rico, and we went over with him what we had done, through many discussions and many clarifications. When I returned to New York, I brought with me an almost-finished version of the book; and there, Padilla and I would meet one day a week, sit with a desk between us, and go over the poems, line by line. It was exhilarating, for our differences usually generated wandering conversations, the very antithesis of the monkish immersion of working alone. Similarly, Andrew Hurley and I found that, in many cases, our separate versions of the same line in Spanish would together yield up a better third. We also made a point of reading the poems aloud to each other, so that we always remained aware of the dimension of sound and did not have to hear the poems in our heads.

When Padilla's book was lodged with the publisher, he and I went on meeting one day a week, for he had undertaken to translate, for a Spanish publisher, a selection of my poems and a long autobiographical prose piece I had written. We continued to work across the desk, but with the difference that it was I who wagged fingers, or cried out occasionally, in pain or in enthusiasm. So much gets turned up in the course of a translation that we made many discoveries, and would even keep notes of our more brilliant errors; and, inevitably, I learned more Spanish, Heberto more English. We were neither of us strangers to solitary translation, and we discovered that working together, out loud, both energised and delighted us. Padilla referred to our collaborative translation as '*la mutualidad*', and it was a pleasure, not at all a pain.

I had two similar experiences, one with José Emilio Pacheco, while I was translating a book of his poems; but most of our to-ing and fro-ing had to be done by letter. To have access to the poet, the original, however, and to have him take the meticulous interest that Pacheco did, is a lifeline for a translator. It may spoil him for monkish labour, but it is bound to make for a better result. The other occasion was more exuberant. In London, I worked with Guillermo Cabrera Infante – he was an old friend of mine, and we were almost neighbours – on making versions of some of his stories for *The New Yorker*. Guillermo was a master of the untranslatable. He was also so agile in both Spanish and English that there were virtually two of him. Quite often, he would bend the language of the original for a better effect in English, and our working sessions were both heady and hilarious. We were essentially collaborating on a piece of writing in English, hedge-hopping over the language of the original.

Not all writers take the same interest in their work in translation, so situations like the ones I describe remain almost luxurious exceptions. Pablo Neruda did not bother much about the versions translators made of his poems, for it would have claimed too much of his time. He said to me once, when I was embarking on an English translation of *Estravagario*, with a twinkle, 'Don't just translate my poems, I want you to improve them!' Borges, on the other hand, always so polite and impenetrably modest, professed to like any translated version better than his original, which does not really help a translator, and led him at times to endorse versions of his work that were not first-rate. Mario Vargas Llosa has always taken great pains to scrutinise translations of his books, and such interest on the part of the writer is always a great spur to the translator. I wish it were more readily available.

The point in bringing up these experiences is a simple one: that translation gains a great deal, that the translator finds the work much more rewarding, when he can actively work with someone whose language is the language of the original text, who can act as both caretaker and clarifier of that text. Error is much less likely, and can almost be eliminated. Stylistic mannerisms, allusions and associations do not pass unnoticed. The translator offers up various versions until a satisfactory one is reached by consensus, although, in the case of the translated version, his is the last word. The process, moreover, can work in the opposite linguistic direction. I have more than once worked in this way with a friend from another language, dictating the arrived-at version into a tape recorder, and ending up with a near-finished version on tape, for refinement. This method has yielded me both pleasure and discovery, and is much to be preferred, in my book, to the page-turnings of solitary translating. It also takes much less time. I wish translators would use it more often. I hope some of them will try.

A. R.

What Gets Lost

I keep translating *traduzco continuamente*
entre palabras words *que no son las mias*
into other words which are mine *de palabras a mis palabras.*

Y finalmente de quien es el texto?
Who do words belong to?
Del escritor o del traductor writer, translator
o de los idiomas or to language itself?
Traductores, somos fantasmas que viven
entre aquel mundo y el nuestro
translators are ghosts who live
in a limbo between two worlds
pero poco a poco me ocurre
que el problema no es cuestion
de lo que se pierde en traducion
the problem is not a question
of what gets lost in translation
sino but rather *lo que se pierde*
what gets lost
entre la ocurrencia — sea de amor o de agonia
between the happening of love or pain
y el hecho de que llega
a existir en palabras
and their coming into words.

Para nosotros todos, amantes, habladores
for lovers or users of words
el problema es este this is the difficulty —
lo que se pierde what gets lost
no es lo que se pierde en traducion sino
is not what gets lost in translation but more
what gets lost in language itself *lo que se pierde*
en el hecho en la lengua,
en la palabra misma.

Translator to Poet

For Pablo Neruda, 1904–73

There are only the words left now. They lie like tombstones
or the stone Andes where the green scrub ends.
I do not have the heart to chip away
at your long lists of joy, which alternate
their iron and velvet, all the vegetation
and whalebone of your chosen stormy coast.
So much was written hope, with every line
extending life by saying, every meeting
ending in expectation of the next.
It was your slow intoning voice that counted,
bringing a living Chile into being
where poetry was bread, where books were banquets.
Now they are silent, stony on the shelf.
I cannot read them for the thunderous silence,
the grief of Chile's dying and your own,
death being the one definitive translation.

SELECTED TRANSLATIONS

Jorge Luis Borges

Poem of the Gifts

No one should read self-pity or reproach
into this statement of the majesty
of God, who with such splendid irony
granted me books and blindness at one touch.

Care of this city of books he handed over
to sightless eyes, which now can do no more
than read in libraries of dream the poor
and senseless paragraphs that dawns deliver

to wishful scrutiny. In vain the day
squanders on these same eyes its infinite tomes,
as distant as the inaccessible volumes
that perished once in Alexandria.

From hunger and from thirst (in the Greek story),
a king lies dying among gardens and fountains.
Aimlessly, endlessly, I trace the confines,
high and profound, of this blind library.

Cultures of East and West, the entire atlas,
encyclopedias, centuries, dynasties,
symbols, the cosmos, and cosmogonies
are offered from the walls, all to no purpose.

In shadow, with a tentative stick, I try
the hollow twilight, slow and imprecise –
I, who had always thought of Paradise
in form and image as a library.

Something, which certainly is not defined
by the word *fate*, arranges all these things;
another man was given, on other evenings
now gone, these many books. He too was blind.

Wandering through the gradual galleries,
I often feel with vague and holy dread
I am that other dead one, who attempted
the same uncertain steps on similar days.

Which of the two is setting down this poem –
a single sightless self, a plural I?
What can it matter, then, the name that names me,
given our curse is common and the same?

Groussac* or Borges, now I look upon
this dear world losing shape, fading away
into a pale uncertain ashy-gray
that feels like sleep, or else oblivion.

The Hourglass

It is appropriate that time be measured
by the stark shadow cast by a stake in summer
or by the flow of water in the river
where Heraclitus saw time's ironies

since, seen as time and fate, they are alike:
the movement of the mindless daytime shadow
and the irrevocable running on
of river water following its flow.

Just so, but time discovered in the deserts
another substance, smooth and of some weight,
that seemed to have been specifically imagined
for measuring out the ages of the dead.

---

* Paul Groussac (1845–1929), Argentine critic and man of letters, and a
  predecessor of Borges as director of the National Library, also suffered
  from the accompanying irony of blindness.

And so appears this instrument of legend
in the engravings in the dictionary,
an object graying antiquarians
will banish to a dusty underworld

of things – a single chessman, a broadsword,
now lifeless, and a clouded telescope,
sandalwood worn away by opium,
a world of dust, of chance, of nothingness.

Who has not hesitated, seeing that hourglass,
severe and sombre, in the god's right hand,
accompanying the scythe he also handles,
the image Dürer copied in his drawing?

Through a top opening, the inverted cone
slowly lets fall the wary grains of sand,
a gradual gold that, loosening, fills up
the concave crystal of its universe.

Pleasure there is in watching how the sand
slowly slithers up and makes a slope
then, just about to fall, piles up again
with an insistence that appears quite human.

The sand of every cycle is the same
and infinite is the history of sand;
so, underlying your fortunes and your sorrows,
yawns an invulnerable eternity.

It never stops, the spilling of the sand.
I am the one who weakens, not the glass.
The rite of the falling sand is infinite
and, with the sand, our lives are leaving us.

In the timing of the sand, I seem to feel
a cosmic time: all the long history
that memory keeps sealed up in its mirrors
or that has been dissolved by magic Lethe.

All these: the pillar of smoke, the pillar of fire,
Carthage, Rome, and their constricting wars,
Simon Magus, the seven feet of earth
the Saxon offers the Norwegian king –

all are obliterated, all brought down
by the tireless trickle of the endless sand.
I do not have to save myself – I too
am whim of time, that shifty element.

Chess

I

Set in their studious corners, the players
move the gradual pieces. Until dawn
the chessboard keeps them in its strict confinement
with its two colors set at daggers drawn.

Within the game itself the forms give off
their magic rules: Homeric castle, knight
swift to attack, queen warlike, king decisive,
slanted bishop, and attacking pawns.

Eventually, when the players have withdrawn,
when time itself has finally consumed them,
the ritual certainly will not be done.

It was in the East this war took fire.
Today the whole earth is its theater.
Like the game of love, this game goes on forever.

II

Faint-hearted king, sly bishop, ruthless queen,
straightforward castle, and deceitful pawn –
over the checkered black and white terrain
they seek out and begin their armed campaign.

They do not know it is the player's hand
that dominates and guides their destiny.
They do not know an adamantine fate
controls their will and lays the battle plan.

The player too is captive of caprice
(the words are Omar's) on another ground
where black nights alternate with whiter days.

God moves the player, he in turn the piece.
But what god beyond God begins the round
of dust and time and sleep and agonies?

Mirrors

I have been horrified before all mirrors
not just before the impenetrable glass,
the end and the beginning of that space,
inhabited by nothing but reflections,

but faced with specular water, mirroring
the other blue within its bottomless sky,
incised at times by the illusory flight
of inverted birds, or troubled by a ripple,

or face to face with the unspeaking surface
of ghostly ebony whose very hardness
reflects, as if within a dream, the whiteness
of spectral marble or a spectral rose.

Now, after so many troubling years
of wandering beneath the wavering moon,
I ask myself what accident of fortune
handed to me this terror of all mirrors –

mirrors of metal and the shrouded mirror
of sheer mahogany which in the twilight

of its uncertain red softens the face
that watches and in turn is watched by it.

I look on them as infinite, elemental
fulfillers of a very ancient pact
to multiply the world, as in the act
of generation, sleepless and dangerous.

They extenuate this vain and dubious world
within the web of their own vertigo.
Sometimes at evening they are clouded over
by someone's breath, someone who is not dead.

The glass is watching us. And if a mirror
hangs somewhere on the four walls of my room,
I am not alone. There's an other, a reflection
which in the dawn enacts its own dumb show.

Everything happens, nothing is remembered
in those dimensioned cabinets of glass
in which, like rabbis in fantastic stories,
we read the lines of text from right to left.

Claudius, king for an evening, king in a dream,
did not know he was a dream until that day
on which an actor mimed his felony
with silent artifice, in a tableau.

Strange, that there are dreams, that there are mirrors.
Strange that the ordinary, worn-out ways
of every day encompass the imagined
and endless universe woven by reflections.

God (I've begun to think) implants a promise
in all that insubstantial architecture
that makes light out of the impervious surface
of glass, and makes the shadow out of dreams.

God has created nights well-populated
with dreams, crowded with mirror images,
so that man may feel that he is nothing more
than vain reflection. That's what frightens us.

Rain

Quite suddenly the evening clears at last
as now outside the soft small rain is falling.
Falling or fallen. Rain itself is something
undoubtedly which happens in the past.

Whoever hears it falling has remembered
a time in which a curious twist of fate
brought back to him a flower whose name was 'rose'
and the perplexing redness of its red.

This rain which spreads its blind across the pane
must also brighten in forgotten suburbs
the black grapes on a vine across a shrouded

patio now no more. The evening's rain
brings me the voice, the dear voice of my father,
who comes back now, who never has been dead.

The Other Tiger

> And the craft createth a semblance.
> – Morris, *Sigurd the Volsung* (1876)

I think of a tiger. The fading light enhances
the vast complexities of the Library
and seems to set the bookshelves at a distance;
powerful, innocent, bloodstained, and new-made,
it will prowl through its jungle and its morning
and leave its footprint on the muddy edge
of a river with a name unknown to it
(in its world, there are no names, nor past, nor future,
only the sureness of the present moment)

and it will cross the wilderness of distance
and sniff out in the woven labyrinth
of smells the smell peculiar to morning
and the scent on the air of deer, delectable.
Behind the lattice of bamboo, I notice
its stripes, and I sense its skeleton
under the magnificence of the quivering skin.
In vain the convex oceans and the deserts
spread themselves across the earth between us;
from this one house in a far-off seaport
in South America, I dream you, follow you,
oh tiger on the fringes of the Ganges.

Evening spreads in my spirit and I keep thinking
that the tiger I am calling up in my poem
is a tiger made of symbols and of shadows,
a set of literary images,
scraps remembered from encyclopedias,
and not the deadly tiger, the fateful jewel
that in the sun or the deceptive moonlight
follows its paths, in Bengal or Sumatra,
of love, of indolence, of dying.
Against the tiger of symbols I have set
the real one, the hot-blooded one
that savages a herd of buffalo,
and today, the third of August, '59,
its patient shadow moves across the plain,
but yet, the act of naming it, of guessing
what is its nature and its circumstance
creates a fiction, not a living creature,
not one of those that prowl on the earth.

Let us look for a third tiger. This one
will be a form in my dream like all the others,
a system, an arrangement of human language,
and not the flesh-and-bone tiger
that, out of reach of all mythologies,
paces the earth. I know all this; yet something

drives me to this ancient, perverse adventure,
foolish and vague, yet still I keep on looking
throughout the evening for the other tiger,
the other tiger, the one not in this poem.

The Cyclical Night

To Sylvina Bullrich

They knew it, the fervent pupils of Pythagoras:
that stars and men revolve in a cycle,
that fateful atoms will bring back the vital
gold Aphrodite, Thebans, and agoras.

In future epochs the centaur will oppress
with solid uncleft hoof the breast of the Lapith;
when Rome is dust the Minotaur will moan
once more in the endless dark of its rank palace.

Every sleepless night will come back in minute
detail. This writing hand will be born from the same
womb, and bitter armies contrive their doom.
(Edinburgh's David Hume made this very point.)

I do not know if we will recur in a second
cycle, like numbers in a periodic fraction;
but I know that a vague Pythagorean rotation
night after night sets me down in the world

on the outskirts of this city. A remote street
which might be either north or west or south,
but always with a blue-washed wall, the shade
of a fig tree, and a sidewalk of broken concrete.

This, here, is Buenos Aires. Time, which brings
either love or money to men, hands on to me
only this withered rose, this empty tracery
of streets with names recurring from the past

in my blood: Laprida, Cabrera, Soler, Suárez . . .
names in which secret bugle calls are sounding,
invoking republics, cavalry, and mornings,
joyful victories, men dying in action.

Squares weighed down by a night in no one's care
are the vast patios of an empty palace,
and the single-minded streets creating space
are corridors for sleep and nameless fear.

It returns, the hollow dark of Anaxagoras;
in my human flesh, eternity keeps recurring
and the memory, or plan, of an endless poem beginning:
'They knew it, the fervent pupils of Pythagoras . . . '

Of Heaven and Hell

The Inferno of God is not in need of
the splendor of fire. When, at the end of things,
Judgment Day resounds on the trumpets
and the earth opens and yields up its entrails
and nations reconstruct themselves from dust
to bow before the unappealable Judgment,
eyes then will not see the nine circles
of the inverted mountain, nor the pale
meadow of perennial asphodels
in which the shadow of the archer follows
the shadow of the deer, eternally,
nor the fiery ditch on the lowest level
of the infernos of the Muslim faith,
antedating Adam and the Fall,
nor the violence of metals, nor even
the almost visible blindness of Milton.
No fearful labyrinth of iron,
no doleful fires of suffering, will oppress
the awestruck spirits of the damned.

Nor does the far point of the years conceal
a secret garden. God does not require,
to celebrate the merits of the good life,
globes of light, concentric theories
of thrones and heavenly powers and cherubim,
nor the beguiling mirror that is music,
nor all the many meanings in a rose,
nor the fateful splendor of a single
one of his tigers, nor the subtleties
of a sunset turning gold in the desert,
nor the immemorial, natal taste of water.
In God's infinite care, there are no gardens,
no flash of hope, no glint of memory.

In the clear glass of a dream, I have glimpsed
the Heaven and Hell that lie in wait for us:
when Judgment Day sounds in the last trumpets
and planet and millennium both
disintegrate, and all at once, O Time,
all your ephemeral pyramids cease to be,
the colors and the lines that trace the past
will in the semidarkness form a face,
a sleeping face, faithful, still, unchangeable
(the face of the loved one, or, perhaps, your own)
and the sheer contemplation of that face –
never-changing, whole, beyond corruption –
will be, for the rejected, an Inferno,
and, for the elected, Paradise.

Poem of the Fourth Element

The god, whom a soldier of the line of Atreus
had cornered on a beach burned by the sun,
changed in turn into lion, dragon, panther,
tree, and then water. For water is Proteus.

It is the unrepeatable cloud, the glory
of the sun setting, staining the outskirts red;
it is the Maelstrom turning the glacial whirlpools,
and the useless tear I let fall in your memory.

In the cosmogonies, it was the secret source
of the nourishing earth and the devouring fire,
of the powers that rule the dawn and the west wind.
(Or so claim Seneca and Thales of Miletus.)

The sea and the shift of mountains that destroy
the ships of iron are only your disguises,
and relentless time, that wounds us and moves on,
only another of your metaphors, Water.

Under laboring winds, you were the labyrinth,
windowless, wall-less, whose gray waterways
for long distracted the forlorn Ulysses,
with certain death and vagaries of chance.

You gleam, like the cruel blades of cutlasses,
you take the forms of dreams, nightmares, monsters.
To you the tongues of men attribute wonders.
Your flights are called the Euphrates or the Ganges.

(They claim it is holy, the water of the latter,
but, as the seas work in their secret ways
and the planet is porous, it may still be true
to claim all men have bathed in the Ganges.)

De Quincey, in the tumult of his dreams,
saw your seas strewn with faces and with nations.
You have soothed the anguish of the generations.
You have bathed my father's flesh, and that of Christ.

Water, I ask a favor. Through this indolent
arrangement of measured words I speak to you.
Remember Borges, your friend, who swam in you.
Be present to my lips in my last moment.

Matthew xxv:30

*And cast ye the unprofitable servant into outer darkness:
there shall be weeping and gnashing of teeth.*

The first bridge, Constitution Station. At my feet
the shunting trains trace iron labyrinths.
Steam hisses up and up into the night,
which becomes at a stroke the night of the Last Judgment.

From the unseen horizon
and from the very center of my being,
an infinite voice pronounced these things –
things, not words. This is my feeble translation,
time-bound, of what was a single limitless Word:
'Stars, bread, libraries of East and West,
playing-cards, chessboards, galleries, skylights, cellars,
a human body to walk with on the earth,
fingernails, growing at nighttime and in death,
shadows for forgetting, mirrors busily multiplying,
cascades in music, gentlest of all time's shapes.
Borders of Brazil, Uruguay, horses and mornings,
a bronze weight, a copy of the Grettir Saga,
algebra and fire, the charge at Junín in your blood,

days more crowded than Balzac, scent of the honeysuckle,
love and the imminence of love and intolerable remembering,
dreams like buried treasure, generous luck,
and memory itself, where a glance can make men dizzy –
all this was given to you, and with it
the ancient nourishment of heroes –
treachery, defeat, humiliation.
In vain have oceans been squandered on you, in vain
the sun, wonderfully seen through Whitman's eyes.
You have used up the years and they have used up you,
and still, and still, you have not written the poem.'

Limits

Of all the streets that blur into the sunset,
there must be one (which, I am not sure)
that I by now have walked for the last time
without guessing it, the pawn of that Someone

who fixes in advance omnipotent laws,
sets up a secret and unwavering scale
for all the shadows, dreams, and forms
woven into the texture of this life.

If there is a limit to all things and a measure
and a last time and nothing more and forgetfulness,
who will tell us to whom in this house
we without knowing it have said farewell?

Through the dawning window night withdraws
and among the stacked books that throw
irregular shadows on the dim table,
there must be one which I will never read.

There is in the South more than one worn gate,
with its cement urns and planted cactus,
which is already forbidden to my entry,
inaccessible, as in a lithograph.

There is a door you have closed forever
and some mirror is expecting you in vain;
to you the crossroads seem wide open,
yet watching you, four-faced, is a Janus.

There is among all your memories one
which has now been lost beyond recall.
You will not be seen going down to that fountain,
neither by white sun nor by yellow moon.

You will never recapture what the Persian
said in his language woven with birds and roses,
when, in the sunset, before the light disperses,
you wish to give words to unforgettable things.

And the steadily-flowing Rhone and the lake,
all that vast yesterday over which today I bend?
They will be as lost as Carthage,
scourged by the Romans with fire and salt.

At dawn I seem to hear the turbulent
murmur of crowds milling and fading away;
they are all I have been loved by, forgotten by;
space, time, and Borges now are leaving me.

Readers

Of that gentleman with the sallow, dry complexion
and knightly disposition, they conjecture
that, always on the edge of an adventure,
he never actually left his library.
The precise chronicle of his campaigning
and all its tragicomical reversals
was dreamed by him and not by Cervantes
and is no more than a record of his dreaming.
Such is also my luck. I know there is something
essential and immortal that I have buried
somewhere in that library of the past
in which I read the story of that knight.
The slow leaves now recall a solemn child
who dreams vague things he does not understand.

Waking Up

Daylight leaks in, and sluggishly I surface
from my own dreams into the common dream
and things assume again their proper places
and their accustomed shapes. Into this present
the Past intrudes, in all its dizzying range –
the centuries-old habits of migration
in birds and men, the armies in their legions
all fallen to the sword, and Rome and Carthage.

The trappings of my day also come back:
my voice, my face, my nervousness, my luck.
If only Death, that other waking-up,
would grant me a time free of all memory
of my own name and all that I have been!
If only morning meant oblivion!

To One No Longer Young

Already you can see the tragic setting
and each thing there in its appointed place;
the broadsword and the ash destined for Dido,
the coin ready for Belisarius.
Why do you go on searching in the hazy
bronze of old hexameters for war
when seven feet of ground wait for you here,
the sudden rush of blood, the open grave?
Here watching you is the inscrutable glass
that will dream up and then forget the face
of all your dwindling days, your agonies.
The last one now draws near. It is the house
in which your slow, brief evening comes to pass
and the street that you look at every day.

The Instant

Where are the centuries, where is the dream
of sword-strife that the Tartars entertained,
where are the massive ramparts that they flattened?
Where is the wood of the Cross, the Tree of Adam?

The present is singular. It is memory
that sets up time. Both succession and error
come with the routine of the clock. A year
is no less vanity than is history.

Between dawn and nightfall is an abyss
of agonies, felicities, and cares.
The face that looks back from the wasted mirrors,
the mirrors of night, is not the same face.
The fleeting day is frail and is eternal:
expect no other Heaven, no other Hell.

191

To Whoever Is Reading Me

You are invulnerable. Have they not granted you,
those powers that preordain your destiny,
the certainty of dust? Is not your time
as irreversible as that same river
where Heraclitus, mirrored, saw the symbol
of fleeting life? A marble slab awaits you
which you will not read – on it, already written,
the date, the city, and the epitaph.
Other men too are only dreams of time,
not indestructible bronze or burnished gold;
the universe is, like you, a Proteus.
Dark, you will enter the darkness that awaits you,
doomed to the limits of your traveled time.
Know that in some sense you are already dead.

Everness

One thing alone does not exist – oblivion.
God, who saves the metal, saves the dross
and stores in his prophetic memory
moons that have still to come, moons that have shone.
Everything is there. The thousands of reflections
which between the dawn and the twilight
your face has left behind in many mirrors
and those faces it will go on leaving yet.
And everything is part of that diverse
and mirroring memory, the universe;
there is no end to its exigent corridors
and the doors that close behind you as you go;
only the far side of the sunset's glow
will show you at last the Archetypes and Splendors.

Elegy

Oh destiny of Borges —
to have traversed the various seas of the world
or the same solitary sea under various names,
to have been part of Edinburgh, Zurich, the two Córdobas,
Colombia, and Texas,
to have gone back across the generations
to the ancient lands of forebears,
to Andalucía, to Portugal, to those shires
where Saxon fought with Dane, mingling bloods,
to have wandered the red and peaceful maze of London,
to have grown old in so many mirrors,
to have tried in vain to catch the marble eyes of statues,
to have studied lithographs, encyclopedias, atlases,
to have witnessed the things that all men witness —
death, the weight of dawn, the endless plain
and the intricacy of the stars,
and to have seen nothing, or almost nothing
but the face of a young girl in Buenos Aires,
a face that does not want to be remembered.
Oh destiny of Borges, perhaps no stranger than yours.

Adam Cast Forth

The Garden – was it real or was it dream?
Slow in the hazy light, I have been asking,
almost as a comfort, if the past
belonging to this now unhappy Adam
was nothing but a magic fantasy
of that God I dreamed. Now it is imprecise
in memory, that lucid paradise,
but I know it exists and will persist
though not for me. The unforgiving earth
is my affliction, and the incestuous wars
of Cains and Abels and their progeny.
Nevertheless, it means much to have loved,
to have been happy, to have laid my hand on
the living Garden, even for one day.

Milonga of Manuel Flores

Manuel Flores is doomed to die.
That's as sure as your money.
Dying is a custom
well-known to many.

But even so, it pains me
to say goodbye to living,
that state so well-known now,
so sweet, so solid-seeming.

I look at my hand in the dawning.
I look at the veins contained there.
I look at them in amazement
as I would look at a stranger.

Tomorrow comes the bullet,
oblivion descending.
Merlin the magus said it:
being born has an ending.

So much these eyes have seen,
such things, such places!
Who knows what they will see
when I've been judged by Jesus.

Manuel Flores is doomed to die.
That's as sure as your money.
Dying is a custom
well-known to many.

Tankas

I

High on the summit,
the garden is all moonlight,
the moon is golden.
More precious is the contact
of your lips in the shadow.

2

The sound of a bird
which the twilight is hiding
has fallen silent.
You pace the garden.
I know that you miss something.

3

The curious goblet,
the sword which was a sword once
in another grasp,

the moonlight on the street –
tell me, are they not enough?

4

Underneath the moon,
tiger of gold and shadow
looks down at his claws,
unaware that in the dawn
they lacerated a man.

5

Wistful is the rain
falling upon the marble,
sad to become earth,
sad no longer to be part
of man, of dream, of morning.

6

Not to have fallen,
like others of my lineage,
cut down in battle.
To be in the fruitless night
he who counts the syllables.

1971

Two men walked on the surface of the moon.
Others will, later. What are words to do?
And what of the dreams and fashionings of art
before this real, almost unreal, event?
Heady with daring and with holy dread,
those sons of Whitman now have left their print
on the moon's wasteland, the unviolated
prehuman sphere, changing and permanent.
The love of Endymion in his mountain vigil,
the hippogriff, the curious sphere of Wells,
which in my memory is real and true,
now all take substance. Triumph belongs to all.
Today there is not a single man on earth
who does not feel more confident, more sure.
The unforgettable day thrills with new force
from the single rightness of the odyssey
of those benign magicians. The moon,
which earthly love still seeks out in the sky
with sorrowing face and still-unslaked desire,
will be its monument, everlasting, one.

The Watcher

The light enters and I remember who I am; he is there.
He begins by telling me his name which (it should now be clear)
     is mine.
I revert to the servitude which has lasted more than seven times
     ten years.
He saddles me with his rememberings.
He saddles me with the miseries of every day, the human condition.
I am his old nurse; he requires me to wash his feet.
He spies on me in mirrors, in mahogany, in shop windows.
One or another woman has rejected him, and I must share his
     anguish.
He dictates to me now this poem, which I do not like.
He insists I apprentice myself tentatively to the stubborn Anglo-
     Saxon.
He has won me over to the hero worship of dead soldiers,
people with whom I could scarcely exchange a single word.
On the last flight of stairs, I feel him at my side.
He is in my footsteps, in my voice.
Down to the last detail, I abhor him.
I am gratified to remark that he can hardly see.
I am in a circular cell and the infinite wall is closing in.
Neither of the two deceives the other, but we both lie.
We know each other too well, inseparable brother.
You drink the water from my cup and you wolf down my bread.
The door to suicide is open, but theologians assert that, in the
subsequent shadows of the other kingdom, there will I be,
waiting for myself.

1891

I catch a glimpse of him and then I lose him –
best black suit well-brushed and narrow-fitting,
nondescript neckerchief around the throat,
narrow forehead, straggling moustache,
he walks among the people of the evening,
lost in himself, not seeing anyone.
At a corner counter on the Calle Piedras
he takes a shot of spirits, out of habit.
Someone calls out to him. He doesn't answer.
Behind his eyes, an old resentment smolders.
Another block. A fragment of milonga
falls from a patio. Those cheap guitars
keep gnawing at the edges of his temper,
but still, his walk keeps time, unconsciously.
He lifts his hand and pats the solid handle
of the dagger in the collar of his waistcoat.
He goes to reclaim a debt. It is not far.
A few steps, and the man stops in his walking.
In the passageway, there is a flowering thistle.
He hears the clunk of a bucket in the cistern
and a voice already too well known to him.
He pushes the far door, which is already open
as though he were expected. This very evening
perhaps they will have shown him his own death.

The Palace

The Palace is not infinite.

The walls, the ramparts, the gardens, the labyrinths, the stair-cases, the terraces, the parapets, the doors, the galleries, the circular or rectangular patios, the cloisters, the intersections, the cisterns, the anterooms, the chambers, the alcoves, the libraries, the attics, the dungeons, the sealed cells and the vaults, are not less in quantity than the grains of sand in the Ganges, but their number has a limit. From the roofs, toward sunset, many people can make out the forges, the workshops, the stables, the boatyards, and the huts of the slaves.

It is granted to no one to traverse more than an infinitesimal part of the palace. Some know only the cellars. We can take in some faces, some voices, some words, but what we perceive is of the feeblest. Feeble and precious at the same time. The date which the chisel engraves in the tablet, and which is recorded in the parochial registers, is later than our own death; we are already dead when nothing touches us, neither a word nor a yearning nor a memory. I know that I am not dead.

The Suicide

Not a single star will be left in the night.
The night will not be left.
I will die and, with me,
the weight of the intolerable universe.
I shall erase the pyramids, the medallions,
the continents and faces.
I shall erase the accumulated past.
I shall make dust of history, dust of dust.
Now I am looking on the final sunset.
I am hearing the last bird.
I bequeath nothingness to no one.

A Blind Man

I do not know what face is looking back
whenever I look at the face in the mirror;
I do not know what old face seeks its image
in silent and already weary anger.
Slow in my blindness, with my hand I feel
the contours of my face. A flash of light
gets through to me. I have made out your hair,
color of ash and at the same time, gold.
I say again that I have lost no more
than the inconsequential skin of things.
These wise words come from Milton, and are noble,
but then I think of letters and of roses.
I think, too, that if I could see my features,
I would know who I am, this precious afternoon.

Talismans

A copy of the first edition of the *Edda Islandorum*, by Snorri, printed in Denmark.

The five volumes of the work of Schopenhauer.

The two volumes of Chapman's *Odyssey*.

A sword which fought in the desert.

A maté gourd with serpent feet which my great-grandfather brought from Lima.

A crystal prism.

A few eroded daguerreotypes.

A terraqueous wooden globe which Cecilia Ingenieros gave me and which belonged to her father.

A stick with a curved handle with which I walked on the plains of America, in Colombia and in Texas.

Various metal cylinders with diplomas.

The gown and mortarboard of a doctorate.

Las Empresas, by Saavedra Fajardo, bound in good-smelling Spanish board.

The memory of a morning.

Lines of Virgil and Frost.

The voice of Macedonio Fernández.

The love or the conversation of a few people.

Certainly they are talismans, but useless against the dark I cannot name, the dark I must not name.

Fame

To have seen Buenos Aires grow, grow and decline.
To recall the earthen patio, the vine, the entryway, the cistern.
To have inherited English, to have delved into Anglo-Saxon.
To avow a love of German, a nostalgia for Latin.
To have talked in the Palermo barrio with an old murderer.
To be grateful for chess and jasmine, tigers and hexameters.
To read Macedonio Fernández, in his remembered voice.
To be familiar with the renowned uncertainties of metaphysics.
To have honored the sword and to have a modest love of peace.
Not to have been covetous of islands.
Not to have left my library.
To be Alonso Quijano and not to dare to be Don Quixote.
To have taught what I do not know to those who know more
    than I.
To be grateful for the gifts of the moon and Paul Verlaine.
To have turned some hendecasyllables.
To have gone back to telling old stories.
To have recreated in the language of our day the five or six
    metaphors.
To have avoided bribes.
To be a citizen of Geneva, of Montevideo, of Austin, and (as all
    men are) of Rome.
To be devoted to Conrad.
To be what nobody can define: Argentine.
To be blind.
None of these things is exceptional, yet their coexistence brings
    me a fame I have yet to understand.

The Just

A man who cultivates his garden, as Voltaire wished.
He who is grateful for the existence of music.
He who takes pleasure in tracing an etymology.
Two workmen playing, in a café in the South, a silent game of
    chess.
The potter, contemplating a color and a form.
The typographer who sets this page well, though it may not
    please him.
A woman and a man, who read the last tercets of a certain canto.
He who strokes a sleeping animal.
He who justifies, or wishes to, a wrong done him.
He who is grateful for the existence of Stevenson.
He who prefers others to be right.
These people, unaware, are saving the world.

Elegy for a Park

The labyrinth has vanished. Vanished also
those orderly avenues of eucalyptus,
the summer awnings, and the watchful eye
of the ever-seeing mirror, duplicating
every expression on every human face,
everything brief and fleeting. The stopped clock,
the ingrown tangle of the honeysuckle,
the garden arbor with its whimsical statues,
the other side of evening, the trill of birds,
the mirador, the lazy swish of a fountain,
are all things of the past. Things of what past?
If there were no beginning, nor imminent ending,
if lying in store for us is an infinity
of white days alternating with black nights,
we are living now the past we will become.
We are time itself, the indivisible river.
We are Uxmal and Carthage, we are the perished
walls of the Romans and the vanished park,
the vanished park these lines commemorate.

The Web

Which of my cities will I die in?
Geneva, where revelation came to me
through Virgil and Tacitus, certainly not from Calvin?
Montevideo, where Luis Melian Lafinur,
blind and heavy with years, died among the archives
of that impartial history of Uruguay
he never wrote?
Nara, where in a Japanese inn
I slept on the floor and dreamed the terrible
image of Buddha I had touched sightlessly

but saw in my dream?
Buenos Aires, where I'm almost a foreigner,
given my many years, or else a habitual target
for autograph hunters?
Austin, Texas, where my mother and I
in the autumn of '61 discovered America?
Others will know it too and will forget it.
What language am I doomed to die in?
The Spanish my ancestors used
to call for the charge or bid at truco?
The English of that Bible
my grandmother read from at the desert's edge?
Others will know it too and will forget it.
What time will it be?
In the dove-colored twilight when color fades away
or in the twilight of the crow
when night abstracts and simplifies
all visible things, or at an odd moment –
two in the afternoon?
Others will know it too and will forget it.
These questions are digressions, not from fear
but from impatient hope,
part of the fatal web of cause and effect
that no man can foresee, nor any god.

Pablo Neruda

I ask for silence

Now they leave me in peace.
Now they grow used to my absence.

I am going to close my eyes.

I only want five things,
five chosen roots.

One is an endless love.

Two is to see the autumn.
I cannot exist without leaves
flying and falling to earth.

The third is the solemn winter,
the rain I loved, the caress
of fire in the rough cold.

My fourth is the summer,
plump as a watermelon.

And fifthly, your eyes.
Matilde, my dear love,
I will not sleep without your eyes,
I will not exist but in your gaze.
I adjust the spring
for you to follow me with your eyes.

That, friends, is all I want.
Next to nothing, close to everything.

Now they can go if they wish.

I have lived so much that some day
they will have to forget me forcibly,
rubbing me off the blackboard.
My heart was inexhaustible.

But because I ask for silence,
don't think I'm going to die.
The opposite is true;
it happens I'm going to live.

To be, and to go on being.

I will not be, however, if, inside me,
the crop does not keep sprouting,
the shoots first, breaking through the earth
to reach the light;
but the mothering earth is dark,
and, deep inside me, I am dark.
I am a well in the water of which
the night leaves stars behind
and goes on alone across fields.

It's a question of having lived so much
that I want to live that much more.

I never felt my voice so clear,
never have been so rich in kisses.

Now, as always, it is early.
The light is a swarm of bees.

Let me alone with the day.
I ask leave to be born.

PABLO NERUDA

Keeping quiet

Now we will count to twelve
and we will all keep still.

For once on the face of the earth,
let's not speak in any language;
let's stop for one second,
and not move our arms so much.

It would be an exotic moment
without rush, without engines;
we would all be together
in a sudden strangeness.

Fishermen in the cold sea
would not harm whales
and the man gathering salt
would look at his hurt hands.

Those who prepare green wars,
wars with gas, wars with fire,
victories with no survivors,
would put on clean clothes
and walk about with their brothers
in the shade, doing nothing.

What I want should not be confused
with total inactivity.
Life is what it is about;
I want no truck with death.

If we were not so single-minded
about keeping our lives moving,
and for once could do nothing,
perhaps a huge silence
might interrupt this sadness

of never understanding ourselves
and of threatening ourselves with death.
Perhaps the earth can teach us
as when everything seems dead
and later proves to be alive.

Now I'll count up to twelve
and you keep quiet and I will go.

The great tablecloth

When they were called to the table,
the tyrants came rushing
with their temporary ladies;
it was fine to watch the women pass
like wasps with big bosoms
followed by those pale
and unfortunate public tigers.

The farmer in the field ate
his poor quota of bread,
he was alone, it was late,
he was surrounded by wheat,
but he had no more bread;
he ate it with grim teeth,
looking at it with hard eyes.

In the blue hour of eating,
the infinite hour of the roast,
the poet abandons his lyre,
takes up his knife and fork,
puts his glass on the table,
and the fishermen attend

the little sea of the soup bowl.
Burning potatoes protest
among the tongues of oil.
The lamb is gold on its coals
and the onion undresses.
It is sad to eat in dinner clothes,
like eating in a coffin,
but eating in convents
is like eating underground.
Eating alone is a disappointment,
but not eating matters more,
is hollow and green, has thorns
like a chain of fish hooks
trailing from the heart,
clawing at your insides.

Hunger feels like pincers,
like the bite of crabs,
it burns, burns and has no fire.
Hunger is a cold fire.
Let us sit down soon to eat
with all those who haven't eaten;
let us spread great tablecloths,
put salt in the lakes of the world,
set up planetary bakeries,
tables with strawberries in snow,
and a plate like the moon itself
from which we can all eat.

For now I ask no more
than the justice of eating.

Fear

Everyone is after me to exercise,
get in shape, play football,
rush about, even go swimming and flying.
Fair enough.

Everyone is after me to take it easy.
They all make doctor's appointments for me,
eyeing me in that quizzical way.
What is going on?

Everyone is after me to take a trip,
to come in, to leave, not to travel,
to die and, alternatively, not to die.
It doesn't matter.

Everyone is spotting oddnesses
in my innards, suddenly shocked
by radio-awful diagrams.
I don't agree with them.

Everyone is picking at my poetry
with their relentless knives and forks,
trying, no doubt, to find a fly.
I am afraid.

I am afraid of the whole world,
afraid of cold water, afraid of death.
I am as all mortals are,
unable to be patient.

And so, in these brief, passing days,
I shall not take them into account.
I shall open up and imprison myself
with my most treacherous enemy,
Pablo Neruda.

How much happens in a day

In the course of a day we shall meet one another.

But, in one day, things spring to life –
they sell grapes in the street,
tomatoes change their skin,
the young girl you wanted
never came back to the office.

They changed the postman suddenly.
The letters now are not the same.
A few golden leaves and it's different;
this tree is now well off.

Who would have said that the earth
with its ancient skin would change so much?
It has more volcanoes than yesterday,
the sky has brand-new clouds,
the rivers are flowing differently.
Besides, so much has come into being!
I have inaugurated hundreds
of highways and buildings,
delicate, clean bridges
like ships or violins.

And so, when I greet you
and kiss your flowering mouth,
our kisses are other kisses,
our mouths are other mouths.

Joy, my love, joy in all things,
in what falls and what flourishes.

Joy in today and yesterday,
the day before and tomorrow.

Joy in bread and stone,

joy in fire and rain.

In what changes, is born, grows,
consumes itself, and becomes a kiss again.

Joy in the air we have,
and in what we have of earth.

When our life dries up,
only the roots remain to us,
and the wind is cold like hate.

Then let us change our skin,
our nails, our blood, our gazing;
and you kiss me and I go out
to sell light on the roads.

Joy in the night and the day,
and the four stations of the soul.

Horses

From the window I saw the horses.

I was in Berlin, in winter. The light
was without light, the sky skyless.

The air white like a moistened loaf.

From my window, I could see a deserted arena,
a circle bitten out by the teeth of winter.

All at once, led out by a single man,
ten horses were stepping, stepping into the snow.

Scarcely had they rippled into existence
like flame, than they filled the whole world of my eyes,
empty till now. Faultless, flaming,

they stepped like ten gods on broad, clean hoofs,
their manes recalling a dream of salt spray.

Their rumps were globes, were oranges.

Their colour was amber and honey, was on fire.

Their necks were towers
carved from the stone of pride,
and in their furious eyes, sheer energy
showed itself, a prisoner inside them.

And there, in the silence, at the mid–
point of the day, in a dirty, disgruntled winter,
the horses' intense presence was blood,
was rhythm, was the beckoning light of all being.

I saw, I saw, and seeing, I came to life.
There was the unwitting fountain, the dance of gold, the sky,
the fire that sprang to life in beautiful things.

I have obliterated that gloomy Berlin winter.

I shall not forget the light from these horses.

We are many

Of the many men who I am, who we are,
I can't find a single one;
they disappear among my clothes,
they've left for another city.

When everything seems to be set
to show me off as intelligent,
the fool I always keep hidden
takes over all that I say.

At other times, I'm asleep
among distinguished people,
and when I look for my brave self,
a coward unknown to me
rushes to cover my skeleton
with a thousand fine excuses.

When a decent house catches fire,
instead of the fireman I summon,
an arsonist bursts on the scene,
and that's me. What can I do?
What can I do to distinguish myself?
How can I pull myself together?

All the books I read
are full of dazzling heroes,
always sure of themselves.
I die with envy of them;
and in films full of wind and bullets,
I goggle at the cowboys,
I even admire the horses.

But when I call for a hero,
out comes my lazy old self;
so I never know who I am,

nor how many I am or will be.
I'd love to be able to touch a bell
and summon the real me,
because if I really need myself,
I mustn't disappear.

While I am writing, I'm far away;
and when I come back, I've gone.
I would like to know if others
go through the same things that I do,
if there are many like me;
and when I've exhausted this problem,
I'm going to study so hard
that when I explain myself,
I will talk about geography.

The old women of the shore

To the grave sea come the old women
with shawls knotted round them,
on frail and brittle feet.

They sit themselves on the shore
without changing eyes or hands,
without changing clouds or silence.

The obscene sea breaks and scrapes,
slides down trumpeting mountains,
shakes out its bulls' beards.

The unruffled women sitting
as though in a glass boat
look at the savaging waves.

Where are they going, where have they been?
They come from every corner,
they come from our own life.

Now they have the ocean,
the cold and burning emptiness,
the solitude full of flames.

They come out of all the past,
from houses which once were fragrant,
from burnt-out twilights.

They watch or don't watch the sea,
they scrawl marks with a stick,
and the sea wipes out their calligraphy.

The old women rise and go
on their delicate birds' feet,
while the great roistering waves
roll nakedly on in the wind.

Consequences

He was good, the man, sure
as his hoe and his plough.
He didn't even have time
to dream while he slept.

He was poor to the point of sweat.
He was worth a single horse.

His son today is very proud
and is worth a number of cars.

He speaks with a senator's voice,
he walks with an ample step,
has forgotten his peasant father
and discovered ancestors.
He thinks like a fat newspaper,
makes money night and day,
is important even asleep.

The sons of the son are many,
they married some time ago.
They do nothing, but they consume.
They're worth thousands of mice.

The sons of the sons of the son –
what will they make of the world?
Will they turn out good or bad?
Worth flies or worth wheat?

You don't want to answer me.

But the questions do not die.

Where can Guillermina be?

Where can Guillermina be?

When my sister invited her
and I went out to open the door,
the sun came in, the stars came in,
two tresses of wheat came in
and two inexhaustible eyes.

I was fourteen years old,
brooding, and proud of it,
slim, lithe and frowning,
funereal and formal.
I lived among the spiders,
dank from the forest,
the beetles knew me,
and the three-coloured bees.
I slept among partridges,
hidden under the mint.

Then Guillermina entered
with her blue lightning eyes
which swept across my hair
and pinned me like swords
against the wall of winter.
That happened in Temuco,
there in the South, on the frontier.

The years have passed slowly,
pacing like pachiderms,
barking like crazy foxes.
The soiled years have passed,
waxing, worn, funereal,
and I walked from cloud to cloud,
from land to land, from eye to eye,
while the rain on the frontier
fell in its same grey shape.

My heart has travelled
in the same pair of shoes,
and I have digested the thorns.
I had no rest where I was:
where I hit out, I was struck,
where they murdered me, I fell;
and I revived, as fresh as ever,
and then and then and then and then –
it all takes so long to tell.

I have nothing to add.

I came to live in this world.

Where can Guillermina be?

Sweetness, always

Why such harsh machinery?
Why, to write down the stuff
and people of every day,
must poems be dressed up in gold,
in old and fearful stone?

I want verses of felt or feather
which scarcely weigh, mild verses
with the intimacy of beds
where people have loved and dreamed.
I want poems stained
by hands and everydayness.

Verses of pastry which melt
into milk and sugar in the mouth,
air and water to drink,
the bites and kisses of love.
I long for eatable sonnets,
poems of honey and flour.

Vanity keeps prodding us
to lift ourselves skyward
or to make deep and useless
tunnels underground.
So we forget the joyous
love-needs of our bodies.
We forget about pastries.
We are not feeding the world.

In Madras a long time since,
I saw a sugary pyramid,
a tower of confectionery –
one level after another,
and in the construction, rubies,

and other blushing delights,
medieval and yellow.

Someone dirtied his hands
to cook up so much sweetness.

Brother poets from here
and there, from earth and sky,
from Medellín, from Veracruz,
Abyssinia, Antofagasta,
do you know the recipe for honeycombs?

Let's forget about all that stone.

Let your poetry fill up
the equinoctial pastry shop
our mouths long to devour –
all the children's mouths
and the poor adults' also.
Don't go on without seeing,
relishing, understanding
all these hearts of sugar.

Don't be afraid of sweetness.

With us or without us,
sweetness will go on living
and is infinitely alive,
forever being revived,
for it's in a man's mouth,
whether he's eating or singing,
that sweetness has its place.

The citizen

I went into the toolshops
in all innocence
to buy a simple hammer
or some vague scissors.
I should never have done it.
Since then and restlessly
I devote my time to steel,
to the most shadowy tools:
hoes bring me to my knees,
horseshoes enslave me.

I am troubled all week,
chasing aluminium clouds,
elaborate screws,
bars of silent nickel,
unnecessary door-knockers,
and now the toolshops
are aware of my addiction –
they see me come into the cave
with my wild madman's eyes
and see that I pine for
curious smoky things
which no one would want to buy
and which I only goggle at.

For in the addict's dream
sprout stainless steel flowers,
endless iron blades,
eye-droppers of oil,
water-dippers of zinc,
saws of marine cut.
It's like the inside of a star,
the light in these toolshops –
there in their own splendour

are the essential nails,
the invincible latchkeys,
the bubbles in spirit levels
and the tangles of wire.

They have a whale's heart,
these toolshops of the port –
they've swallowed all the seas,
all the bones of ships,
waves and ancient tides
come together there
and leave behind in that stomach
barrels which rumble about,
ropes like gold arteries,
anchors as heavy as planets,
long and intricate chains
like intestines of the whale itself
and harpoons it swallowed, swimming
east from the Gulf of Penas.

Once I entered, I never left
and never stopped going back;
and I've never got away from
the aura of toolshops.
It's like my home ground,
it teaches me useless things,
it drowns me like nostalgia.

What can I do? There are single men
in hotels, in bachelor rooms;
there are patriots with drums
and inexhaustible fliers
who rise and fall in the air.

I am not in your world.
I'm a dedicated citizen,
I belong to the toolshops.

Too many names

Mondays are meshed with Tuesdays
and the week with the whole year.
Time cannot be cut
with your exhausted scissors,
and all the names of the day
are washed out by the waters of night.

No one can claim the name of Pedro,
nobody is Rosa or María,
all of us are dust or sand,
all of us are rain under rain.
They have spoken to me of Venezuelas,
of Chiles and Paraguays;
I have no idea what they are saying.
I know only the skin of the earth
and I know it has no name.

When I lived amongst the roots
they pleased me more than flowers did,
and when I spoke to a stone
it rang like a bell.

It is so long, the spring
which goes on all winter.
Time lost its shoes.
A year lasts four centuries.

When I sleep every night,
What am I called or not called?
And when I wake, who am I
if I was not I while I slept?

This means to say that scarcely
have we landed into life
than we come as if new-born;
let us not fill our mouths

with so many faltering names,
with so many sad formalities,
with so many pompous letters,
with so much of yours and mine,
with so much signing of papers.

I have a mind to confuse things,
unite them, make them new-born,
mix them up, undress them,
until all light in the world
has the oneness of the ocean,
a generous, vast wholeness,
a crackling, living fragrance.

Through a closed mouth the flies enter

Why, with those red flames at hand,
are rubies so ready to burn?

Why does the heart of the topaz
reveal a yellow honeycomb?

Why does the rose amuse itself
changing the colour of its dreams?

Why does the emerald shiver
like a drowned submarine?

Why does the sky grow pale
under the June stars?

Where does the lizard's tail
get its fresh supply of paint?

Where is the underground fire
that revives the carnations?

Where does the salt acquire
the transparency of its glance?

Where did the coal sleep
that it awoke so dark?

And where, where does the tiger buy
its stripes of mourning, its stripes of gold?

When did the jungle begin
to breathe its own perfume?

When did the pine tree realise
its own sweet-smelling consequence?

When did the lemons learn
the same laws as the sun?

When did smoke learn to fly?

When do roots converse?

What is water like in the stars?
Why is the scorpion poisonous,
the elephant benign?

What is the tortoise brooding on?
Where does shade withdraw to?
What song does the rain repeat?
When are the birds going to die?
And why should leaves be green?

What we know is so little,
and what we presume so much,
so slowly do we learn
that we ask questions, then die.
Better for us to keep our pride
for the city of the dead
on the day of the departed,
and there, when the wind blows through
the holes in your skull,
it will unveil to you such mysteries,
whispering the truth to you
through the spaces that were your ears.

Lazybones

They will continue wandering,
these things of steel among the stars,
and worn-out men will still go up
to brutalise the placid moon.
There, they will found their pharmacies.

In this time of the swollen grape,
the wine begins to come to life
between the sea and the mountain ranges.

In Chile now, cherries are dancing,
the dark, secretive girls are singing,
and in guitars, water is shining.

The sun is touching every door
and making wonder of the wheat.

The first wine is pink in colour,
is sweet with the sweetness of a child,
the second wine is able-bodied,
strong like the voice of a sailor,
the third wine is a topaz, is
a poppy and a fire in one.

My house has both the sea and the earth,
my woman has great eyes
the colour of wild hazelnut,
when night comes down, the sea
puts on a dress of white and green,
and later the moon in the spindrift foam
dreams like a sea-green girl.

I have no wish to change my planet.

The Word

The word
was born in the blood,
grew in the dark body, beating,
and took flight through the lips and the mouth.

Farther away and nearer
still, still it came
from dead fathers and from wandering races,
from lands which had turned to stone,
lands weary of their poor tribes,
for when grief took to the roads
the people set out and arrived
and married new land and water
to grow their words again.
And so this is the inheritance;
this is the wavelength which connects us
with dead men and the dawning
of new beings not yet come to light.

Still the atmosphere quivers
with the first word uttered
dressed up
in terror and sighing.
It emerged
from the darkness
and until now there is no thunder
that ever rumbles with the iron voice
of that word,
the first
word uttered —
perhaps it was only a ripple, a single drop,
and yet its great cataract falls and falls.

Later on, the word fills with meaning.
Always with child, it filled up with lives.

Everything was births and sounds –
affirmation, clarity, strength,
negation, destruction, death –
the verb took over all the power
and blended existence with essence
in the electricity of its grace.

Human word, syllable, flank
of extending light and solid silverwork,
hereditary goblet which receives
the communications of the blood –
here is where silence came together with
the wholeness of the human word,
and, for human beings, not to speak is to die –
language extends even to the hair,
the mouth speaks without the lips moving,
all of a sudden, the eyes are words.

I take the word and pass it through my senses
as though it were no more than a human shape;
its arrangements awe me and I find my way
through each resonance of the spoken word –
I utter and I am and, speechless, I approach
across the edge of words silence itself.

I drink to the word, raising
a word or a shining cup;
in it I drink
the pure wine of language
or inexhaustible water,
maternal source of words,
and cup and water and wine
give rise to my song
because the verb is the source
and vivid life – it is blood,
blood which expresses its substance
and so ordains its own unwinding.
Words give glass quality to glass, blood to blood,
and life to life itself.

Births

We will never have any memory of dying.

We were so patient
about our being,
noting down
numbers, days,
years and months,
hair, and the mouths we kiss,
and that moment of dying
we let pass without a note –
we leave it to others as memory,
or we leave it simply to water,
to water, to air, to time.
Nor do we even keep
the memory of being born,
although to come into being was tumultuous and new;
and now you don't remember a single detail
and haven't kept even a trace
of your first light.

It's well known that we are born.

It's well known that in the room
or in the wood
or in the shelter in the fishermen's quarter
or in the rustling canefields
there is a quite unusual silence,
a grave and wooden moment as
a woman prepares to give birth.

It's well known that we were all born.

But of that abrupt translation
from not being to existing, to having hands,
to seeing, to having eyes,

to eating and weeping and overflowing
and loving and loving and suffering and suffering,
of that transition, that quivering
of an electric presence, raising up
one body more, like a living cup,
and of that woman left empty,
the mother who is left there in her blood
and her lacerated fullness,
and its end and its beginning, and disorder
tumbling the pulse, the floor, the covers
till everything comes together and adds
one knot more to the thread of life,
nothing, nothing remains in your memory
of the savage sea which summoned up a wave
and plucked a shrouded apple from the tree.

The only thing you remember is your life.

Goodbyes

Goodbye, goodbye, to one place or another,
to every mouth, to every sorrow,
to the insolent moon, to weeks
which wound in the days and disappeared,
goodbye to this voice and that one stained
with amaranth, and goodbye
to the usual bed and plate,
to the twilit setting of all goodbyes,
to the chair that is part of the same twilight,
to the way made by my shoes.

I spread myself, no question;
I turned over whole lives,
changed skin, lamps, and hates,
it was something I had to do,

not by law or whim,
more of a chain reaction;
each new journey enchained me;
I took pleasure in place, in all places.

And, newly arrived, I promptly said goodbye
with still newborn tenderness
as if the bread were to open and suddenly
flee from the world of the table.
So I left behind all languages,
repeated goodbyes like an old door,
changed cinemas, reasons, and tombs,
left everywhere for somewhere else;
I went on being, and being always
half undone with joy,
a bridegroom among sadnesses,
never knowing how or when,
ready to return, never returning.

It's well known that he who returns never left,
so I traced and retraced my life,
changing clothes and planets,
growing used to the company,
to the great whirl of exile,
to the great solitude of bells tolling.

Alstromeria

In this month of January, the alstromeria,
the flower entombed underground,
comes up out of hiding to the high wastes.
A blush of pink shows in the rock garden.
My eyes take in
its familiar triangle on the sand.
I wonder,

seeing
its pale petal
tooth, the perfect
cradle with its secret spots,
its smooth symmetrical fire –
how did it ready itself underground?
How, when there was nothing there but dust,
rocks, and ashes,
did it sprout, eager, clear, prepared,
protruding its grace into the world?
What was that underground labor like?
When did the form become one with the pollen?
How did the dew seep down
as far as that darkness
and the sudden flower ascend
like a warm flush of fire
till, drop by drop, thread by thread,
the dry places were mantled
and in the rosy light
the air moved, scattering fragrance,
as if from earth alone, dry and deserted,
there had sprung up
a fullness, a flowering,
a freshness multiplied by love?

So did I think in January,
looking at yesterday's dryness; while now,
timidly, crisply grows
the gentle multitude of alstromeria;
and across what once was stone
and dry plain,
the ship of the wind passes, rippling
the fragrant flowering waves.

Past

We have to discard the past
and, as one builds
floor by floor, window by window,
and the building rises,
so do we keep shedding –
first, broken tiles,
then proud doors,
until, from the past,
dust falls
as if it would crash
against the floor,
smoke rises
as if it were on fire,
and each new day
gleams
like an empty
plate.
There is nothing, there was always nothing.
It all has to be filled
with a new, expanding
fruitfulness;
then, down
falls yesterday
as in a well
falls yesterday's water,
into the cistern
of all that is now without voice, without fire.
It is difficult
to get bones used
to disappearing,
to teach eyes
to close,
but

we do it
unwittingly.
Everything was alive,
alive, alive, alive
like a scarlet fish,
but time
passed with cloth and darkness
and kept wiping away
the flash of the fish.
Water water water,
the past goes on falling
although it keeps a grip
on thorns
and on roots.
It went, it went, and now
memories mean nothing.
Now the heavy eyelid
shut out the light of the eye
and what was once alive
is now no longer living;
what we were, we are not.
And with words, although the letters
still have transparency and sound,
they change, and the mouth changes;
the same mouth is now another mouth;
they change, lips, skin, circulation;
another soul took on our skeleton;
what once was in us now is not.
It left, but if they call, we reply
'I am here,' and we realise we are not,
that what was once, was and is lost,
lost in the past, and now does not come back.

Sex

The door at twilight,
in summer.
The last passing carts
of the Indians,
a wavering light
and the smoke
of forest fires
which comes as far as the streets
with the smell of red,
ash
of the distant burning.

I, in mourning,
grave,
withdrawn,
shorts,
thin legs,
knees,
and eyes on the look for
sudden treasures;
Rosita and Josefina
on the other side
of the street,
all teeth and eyes,
full of light, voices
like small, concealed guitars,
calling me.
And I crossed
the street, confused,
terrified;
and hardly
had I arrived
than they whispered to me,
they took my hands,

they covered my eyes
and they ran with me
and my innocence
to the bakehouse.

Silence of great tables, the serious
place of bread, empty of people;
and there, the two of them
and I, prisoner
in the hands of
the first Rosita
and the final Josefina.
They wanted to
undress me.
I fled, trembling,
but I couldn't
run, my legs
couldn't
carry me. Then
the
enchantresses
brought out
before my eyes
a miracle:
the tiny nest
of a small wild bird
with five little eggs,
with five white grapes,
a small
cluster
of forest life,
and I reached out
my hand
while
they fumbled with my clothes,
touched me,
studied with their great eyes

their first small man.

Heavy footsteps, coughing,
my father arriving
with strangers,
and we ran
deep into the dark,
the two pirates
and I, their prisoner,
huddled
among spiderwebs,
squeezed
under a great table, trembling,
while the miracle,
the nest
with its small light-blue eggs,
fell and eventually the intruders' feet
crushed its shape and its fragrance.
But, with the two girls
in the dark,
and fear,
with the smell of flour,
the phantom steps,
the afternoon gradually darkening,
I felt that something was
changing
in my blood
and that to my mouth,
to my hands,
was rising
an electric
flower,
the
hungry,
shining
flower
of desire.

Poetry

And it was at that age ... poetry arrived
in search of me. I don't know, I don't know where
it came from, from winter or a river.
I don't know how or when,
no, they were not voices, they were not
words, not silence,
but from a street it called me,
from the branches of night,
abruptly from the others,
among raging fires
or returning alone,
there it was, without a face,
and it touched me.

I didn't know what to say, my mouth
had no way
with names,
my eyes were blind.
Something knocked in my soul,
fever or forgotten wings,
and I made my own way,
deciphering
that fire,
and I wrote the first, faint line,
faint, without substance, pure
nonsense,
pure wisdom
of someone who knows nothing;
and suddenly I saw
the heavens
unfastened
and open,
planets,

palpitating plantations,
the darkness perforated,
riddled
with arrows, fire, and flowers,
the overpowering night, the universe.

And I, tiny being,
drunk with the great starry
void,
likeness, image of
mystery,
felt myself a pure part
of the abyss.
I wheeled with the stars.
My heart broke loose with the wind.

Bread-Poetry

Poetry, my star-struck patrimony.
It was necessary
to go on discovering, hungry, with no one to guide me,
your earthy endowment,
light of the moon and the secret wheat.

Between solitude and crowds, the key
kept getting lost in streets and in the woods,
under stones, in trains.

The first sign is a state of darkness,
deep rapture in a glass of water,
body stuffed without having eaten,
heart a beggar in its pride.

Many things more that books don't mention,
stuffed as they are with joyless splendor:
to go on chipping at a weary stone,

to go on dissolving the iron in the soul
until you become the person who is reading,
until water finds a voice through your mouth.

And that is easier than tomorrow being Thursday
and yet more difficult than to go on being born –
a strange vocation that seeks you out,
and which goes into hiding when we seek it out,
a shadow with a broken roof
and stars shining through its holes.

Those Lives

This is what I am, I'll say, to leave this written
excuse. This is my life.
Now it is clear this couldn't be done –
that in this net it's not just the strings that count
but also the air that escapes through the meshes.
Everything else stayed out of reach –
time running like a hare
across the February dew,
and love, best not to talk of love
which moved, a swaying of hips,
leaving no more trace of all its fire
than a spoonful of ash.
That's how it is with so many passing things:
the man who waited, believing, of course,
the woman who was alive and will not be.
All of them believed that, having teeth,
feet, hands, and language,
life was only a matter of honor.
This one took a look at history,
took in all the victories of the past,
assumed an everlasting existence,

and the only thing life gave him was
his death, time not to be alive,
and earth to bury him in the end.
But all that was born with as many eyes
as there are planets in the firmament,
and all her devouring fire
ruthlessly devoured her until the end.

If I remember anything in my life,
it was an afternoon in India, on the banks of a river.
They were burning a woman of flesh and bone
and I didn't know if what came from the sarcophagus
was soul or smoke,
until there was neither woman nor fire
nor coffin nor ash. It was late,
and only the night, the water, the river, the darkness
lived on in that death.

October Fullness

Little by little, and also in great leaps,
life happened to me,
and how insignificant this business is.
These veins carried
my blood, which I scarcely ever saw,
I breathed the air of so many places
without keeping a sample of any.
In the end, everyone is aware of this:
nobody keeps any of what he has,
and life is only a borrowing of bones.
The best thing was learning not to have too much
cither of sorrow or of joy,
to hope for the chance of a last drop,
to ask more from honey and from twilight.

Perhaps it was my punishment.
Perhaps I was condemned to be happy.
Let it be known that nobody
crossed my path without sharing my being.
I plunged up to the neck
into adversities that were not mine,
into all the sufferings of others.
It wasn't a question of applause or profit.
Much less. It was not being able
to live or breathe in this shadow,
the shadow of others like towers,
like bitter trees that bury you,
like cobblestones on the knees.

Our own wounds heal with weeping,
our own wounds heal with singing,
but in our own doorway lie bleeding
widows, Indians, poor men, fishermen.
The miner's child doesn't know his father
amidst all that suffering.

So be it, but my business was
the fullness of the spirit:
a cry of pleasure choking you,
a sigh from an uprooted plant,
the sum of all action.

It pleased me to grow with the morning,
to bathe in the sun, in the great joy
of sun, salt, sea-light and wave,
and in that unwinding of the foam
my heart began to move,
growing in that essential spasm,
and dying away as it seeped into the sand.

Dazzle of Day

Enough now of the wet eyes of winter.
Not another single tear.
Hour by hour now, green is beginning,
the essential season, leaf by leaf,
until, in spring's name, we are summoned
to take part in joy.

How wonderful, its eternal all–ness,
new air, the promise of flower,
the full moon leaving
its calling card in the foliage,
men and women trailing back from the beach
with a wet basket
of shifting silver.

Like love, like a medal,
I take in,
take in
south, north, violins,
dogs,
lemons, clay,
newly liberated air.
I take in machines smelling of mystery,
my storm-colored shopping,
everything I need:
orange blossom, string,
grapes like topaz,
the smell of waves.
I gather up,
endlessly,
painlessly,
I breathe.

I dry my clothes in the wind,

and my open heart.
The sky falls
and falls.
From my glass,
I drink
pure joy.

Soliloquy in the Waves

Yes, but here, I am alone.
A wave
builds up,
perhaps it says its name, I don't understand,
mutters, humps in its load
of movement and foam
and withdraws. Who
can I ask what it said to me?
Who among the waves
can I name?
And I wait.

Once again the clearness approached,
the soft numbers
rose in foam
and I didn't know what to call them.
So they whispered away,
seeped into the mouth of the sand.
Time obliterated all lips
with the patience
of shadow and
the orange kiss
of summer.
I stayed alone,
unable to respond to what the world

unquestionably was offering me,
listening to
that richness spreading itself,
the mysterious grapes
of salt, love unknown,
and in the used-up day
only a rumor remained,
further away each time,
until everything that was able to be
changed itself into silence.

The Sea

I need the sea because it teaches me.
I don't know if I learn music or awareness,
if it's a single wave or its vast existence,
or only its harsh voice or its shining one,
a suggestion of fishes and ships.
The fact is that until I fall asleep,
in some magnetic way I move in
the university of the waves.

It's not simply the shells crunched
as if some shivering planet
were giving signs of its gradual death;
no, I reconstruct the day out of a fragment,
the stalactite from a sliver of salt,
and the great god out of a spoonful.

What it taught me before, I keep. It's air,
ceaseless wind, water and sand.

It seems a small thing for a young man,
to have come here to live with his own fire;
nevertheless, the pulse which rose
and fell in its abyss,

the crackling of the blue cold,
the gradual wearing away of the star,
the soft unfolding of the wave
squandering snow with its foam,
the quiet power out there, sure
as a stone shrine in the depths,
replaced my world in which were growing
stubborn sorrow, gathering oblivion,
and my life changed suddenly.
I took the side of pure movement.

Oh, Earth, Wait for Me

Return me, oh sun,
to my country destiny,
rain of the ancient woods.
Bring me back its aroma, and the swords
falling from the sky,
the solitary peace of pasture and rock,
the damp at the river margins,
the smell of the larch tree,
the wind alive like a heart
beating in the crowded remoteness
of the towering araucaria.

Earth, give me back your pristine gifts,
towers of silence which rose from
the solemnity of their roots.
I want to go back to being what I haven't been,
to learn to return from such depths
that among all natural things
I may live or not live. I don't mind
being one stone more, the dark stone,
the pure stone that the river bears away.

PABLO NERUDA

Ars Magnetica

From so much loving and journeying, books emerge.
And if they don't contain kisses or landscapes,
if they don't contain a man with his hands full,
if they don't contain a woman in every drop,
hunger, desire, anger, roads,
they are no use as a shield or as a bell:
they have no eyes, and won't be able to open them,
they have the dead sound of precepts.

I loved the entanglings of genitals,
and out of blood and love I carved my poems.
In hard earth I brought a rose to flower,
fought over by fire and dew.

That's how I could keep on singing.

At Last There Is No One

At last there is no one, no, no voice, no mouth,
no eyes, no hands, no feet; they all went away.
The clean day runs on like a hoop,
the cold air is naked metal.
Yes, metal, air and water, and a yellow
inflorescence, a thick cluster,
and something more, the persistence of its perfume,
pure patrimony of the earth.

Where is the truth? But the key
has got lost in an army of doors,
and it's there among the others,
without
        ever finding
                its lock again.

In the end,
for that reason there is nowhere to lose
the key, nor the truth, nor the lie.

Here
there is no street, no one has a door.
The sand opens up only to a tremor.
And the whole sea opens, the whole of silence,
space with its yellow flowers.
The blind perfume of the earth opens,
and since there are no roads,
no one will come, only
solitude sounding
like the singing of a bell.

Memory

I have to remember everything,
keep track of blades of grass, the threads
of all untidy happenings,
the resting places, inch by inch,
the infinite railroad tracks,
the surfaces of pain.

If I were to misplace one rosebud
and confuse night with a hare,
or even if one whole wall
of my memory were to disintegrate,
I am obliged to make over the air,
steam, earth, leaves,
hair, even the bricks,
the thorns which pierced me,
the speed of flight.

Be gentle with the poet.
I was always quick to forget,
and those hands of mine
could only grasp intangibles,
untouchable things
which could only be compared
when they no longer existed.

The smoke was an aroma,
the aroma something like smoke,
the skin of a sleeping body
which came to life with my kisses;
but don't ask me the date
or the name of what I dreamed –
nor can I measure the road
which may have no country
of that truth that changed

or perhaps turned off by day
to become a wandering light,
a firefly in the dark.

José Emilio Pacheco

High Treason

I do not love my country. Such abstract splendour
is beyond my grasp.
But (although it sounds bad) I would give my life
for ten places in it, for certain people,
seaports, pinewoods, castles,
a run-down city, gray, grotesque,
various figures from its history,
mountains
(and three or four rivers).

Don't Ask Me How The Time Goes By

Winter comes to our venerable house
and across the air pass flocks of migrating birds.
Later, spring will be born again,
the flowers you sowed will come to life.
But we,
we shall never know again
that sweet condition that was ours together.

Roman Conversation

In Rome that poet told me:
You cannot imagine how it saddens me to see you
writing ephemeral prose in magazines.

There are weeds in the Forum. The wind
anoints the pollen with dust.

Under the great marble sun, Rome changes
from ochre to yellow,
to sepia, to bronze.

Everywhere something is breaking down.
Our times are cracking,
It is summer
and you cannot walk through Rome.
So much grandeur enslaved. Chariots
charge against both men and cities.

Companies and phalanxes and legions,
missiles or coffins,
scrap iron,
ruins which will be ruins.

Grasses grow,
fortuitous seeds in the marble.
and garbage in the unremembering streets:
tin cans, paper, scrap.
The consumer's cycle: affluence
is measured by its garbage.

It is hot. We keep on walking,
I have no wish to answer
or to ask myself
if anything written today
will make a mark
any deeper than the pollen in the ruins.

Possibly our verses will last as long
as a 69 Ford
(and certainly not as long as a Volkswagen).

Heberto Padilla

Returning to Bright Places

I have said goodbye to fogged houses
huddled at the edge of mountain passes
like haystacks in Flemish paintings,
said goodbye, too, to the women
who moved me, more than once
— most of all, those with malachite eyes —
and sleds abandoned like gargoyles
in the windows
now shuttered.
For the sun has cured me.
I do not live in remembering any woman,
nor are there countries living in my memory
more intensely than this body resting at my side;
besides, the best ground
for a man to be on
is his own ground, his garden, his own house,
away from the morbid souls who hunt on the docks
the rotten meat of nightmares.
A new day comes in through the window
sparkling, tropical.
The mirror in the room multiplies its brilliance.
I am naked beside my naked woman,
enclosed in this aquarial light;
but this one that hurries across the mirror,
in overcoat and muffler,
rushing downstairs,
hastily greeting the concierge,
going into the crowded dining room
and sitting down to watch
the façade of the train station
like a dunghill
devoured by winter
with its dreary rain —

this is my last reflection,
which now the sun has cured,
the last symptom of that sickness,
thank heaven, transitory.

Song of The Navigator

My invisible amulet against thirteen at table
A gray ship and the great ocean
My lantern of yellow and green lights against fog on the coast
My ox bladder against the cloudy urine of omens
My flint axe
My blue gangway if the hordes return
My soap to counter the lather of shipwrecks
My rosy coral my pistol against rebellions
And my golden bullet
Now – to sea!

Legacies

I don't know if the old people will return one day
at the place we lost them when we were children
I don't think that this is the fate of a dead man; much less
of old people overtaken by the fatigue
of children and grandchildren. Even if they should want it,
they couldn't come back.
The dead must be stubbornly young, wanting to conquer again
the taste of the earth and to push from off them
the weight of the sicknesses that kill them

The dead are sighs and buntings

that sing, my son, my grandmother would tell me
when she still had a piece of time to herself
and could take the time to console me.

The longest-dead have their hands full digging.
They sink downward. They are heavy.
They can't manage to float like the young.
They sink into the ground where we could bury them
and if we got them all together and put them
into coffins, dead, finally, in war,
taken out of the obscene tomb of battles,
still there is no invocation that can wake them.
We can never talk with them or see them
return as then when we had still not left our childhood.
They are better that way, I think – underground.
That way they will never have memory, nostalgia,
never have remorse, as we have.

Houses

I can never avoid, at the most unlikely times,
the vision of houses I lived in as a child.
Some, I remember, were far from ugly, but I didn't love them.
I wanted to build a box-room,
a wooden passageway
with deep hiding places
where I could bury my arrows, my secret stones,
my treasures.
We were always moving from one house to another
(in childhood and ever after).
And what good did that do me?
None at all. I kept them a few years
and then I forgot them.
Porticos, staircases, walls,

knives ruined with rust,
photographs of birthdays and baptisms
start up in my memory,
much like a rush of sea, leaving me salt-stained,
the way waves do.
Shipwrecked houses, lost houses.
Castor, my old sea-dog,
howls all the time from his various corners.

It Is Always The Children
Who Distance Themselves

It is always the children who distance themselves,
their fingers welded to great suitcases
in which their mothers have saved both dreams and horror.

On platforms and in airports
they are taking in everything
as if they were saying 'Where will we go today?'
It is always the children who distance themselves.
To us they are small, invisible, anxious strings.
At night they cling fiercely to our bodies;
but always they distance themselves, jumping about singing
in circles (some of them in tears)
so that not even a father can hear them.

Eugenio Montejo

Two Bodies

How many times, uncertain in the night,
two bodies dream of merging into one,
not knowing they in the end will be three or four.
It happens always at the baring of the ficah
in its eager mystery:
a strange eye opens suddenly on the pillows,
lips meet and cross, flying through the mist,
they suddenly sound, the ill-timed voices
of forgotten lovers.
Mirrors give protection to those spirits
that interrupt the gaspings
and the sighing.
In the alcoves nothing reveals
their cruel and sentimental usurpations.
Only the moon
know which hands are real in their caress,
which faces laugh behind their masks
and which ones out of the embracing shadows
find each other again with furtive steps.
Only the moon, which is full and ample,
soothing and bitter.

In This City

In this city I am a stone;
I am a part of its endless, heavy walls,
Its geometrical silence.

I cannot move. My house falls into ruin.
Buildings collapse, one after another,
rules stretching to the far horizons.

In the depths of the stone I am a lizard,
and in the lizard a yellow stripe,
a stain left by time.

I cannot speak. My tongue entangles me.
Orpheus the stammerer is my companion.
I recognise the barking of his dog.

I am a stone built into the city,
a lizard living in its crevices,
a stripe on its back already very faint.

The days go round and I remain immobile.
I listen still to the beating of my heart,
persistent, in the way that matter moves,
even in the sand that trails from memory,
but I feel only that I do not feel.

Mutations

Mutations by sea, mutations through time itself,
on a ship, in a carriage with books,
changing houses, languages, and landscapes,
partings always, with one staying behind
and another leaving,
Goodbye to a woman's body
which seems now distant, like a distant town
where nights lasted longer than centuries
in lamplight, in hotels.
Mutations out of yourself, out of your own shadow,
in mirrors with deep wells of forgetting
that retain nothing.
Never to be simply
the one who leaves or the one who returns
but something between the two,

something in the middle;
all that life tears from you without its being missed,
all that it brings you that is not a dream,
the lightning bolt that leaves you holding
a cracked stone.

The Flight of Crows

In the newspaper I have opened this morning,
my eyes, my spectacles, can only see
careering armadas of crows
rising and taking flight from page to page.
Feathers blackened by doom-laden news,
a constant cawing covering the earth,
one by one they take the shape of letters,
rising and falling
and coming at times together in banner headlines.
Crows of a rancor printed in cosmic characters,
fluttering between the real world and us,
repetitive crows, crows with errors,
intruding presences, silent, syntactical,
The ink of their wings still wet
and black their blood.

Enrique Lihn

There Are Only Two Countries

There are only two countries: the country of the well, and the
    country of the ill
It is possible for a time to enjoy dual citizenship
but in the long run that becomes meaningless
It hurts to separate off, bit by bit, from the able-bodied to whom
we remain united, until death
but separately united
With the sick a growing complicity springs up
which in no way resembles friendship or love
(those mythologies that yield their last fruits
just before the axe falls)
We begin to exchange messages with our true fellow-citizens
a word of encouragement here
a leaflet on cancer there

A Favorite Little Shrine

I have turned into a little shrine, a favorite
among truck drivers and their families
A little death house lit by candles, devoutly; with fresh flowers
    every day
I have turned into an actor who is going to die, really die, in the
    last act
a famous tightrope walker with no net who dances night after
    night on the loose wire

The telephone in my dressing room rings all the time
They cannot call me to cancel my appearance in the show
they only call to ask me to keep them tickets if only for the third
    act

They call up, people close to my heart, now empty but not
    indifferent,
and people thousands of miles from it
these last ones to make their peace with Jesus, their crutch, by
    way of me
to obtain a last-minute absolution
Par delicatesse I am going to lose, in what is left of my life,
the joy of dying, receiving those bigmouths

Death is a hit with the public
Twelve people are enough for me
I don't want anyone else in the auditorium

The Gift of Dream

The dream makes you the gift of a city you will never set foot in
That longing made unreality
rises up for a fraction of a second, with minarets, squares, and
    fountains
in finer detail
than in a print by Escher
The genie of the dream is an omnipotent architect
No one will ever know the vastness of the cities he has raised for
    a single sick man
condemned in his life never to see Constantinople
a pale shadow before the glory of what
that name brings to his dreams in his dying.

Alvaro Mutis

The most memorable acceptance speech I ever listened to was delivered some ten years ago, in Bogota, Colombia, by the Columbian writer Alvaro Mutis, a dear friend and a superb poet, when he was invested with Columbia's highest cultural decoration, the Cruz de Boyaca, the Cross of Boyaca, in the Palacio Rosado, by the President, who draped the sky-blue sash of the decoration across Alvaro's shoulders. He replied as follows, in my loose translation:

'When I was at school, I discovered that I was incapable of understanding the point of algebra. I saw no reason why x should equal anything other than x, and I resisted, stoically and uncomprehendingly, through several classes, until one day, the algebra master asked me to stay behind. He looked at me for a long time; then he said: "I just don't know what to make of you, Mutis. All I can say is, you'll never win the Cruz de Boyaca." '

A. R.

The Map

I

A scarlet horseman
gallops across the steppes.
His sabre reaches to
the baffled sun,
which waits for him, spread over
a bay bathed in
a tepid silence.

II

Weapons buried in
the thickest part
of the forest
mark the source of a great river.
A wounded warrior
points out the spot, insistently.
His hand stretches to
the desert
and his feet are resting on
an elegant city
with white, sunlit squares.

III

The Great Chief offers
the pipe of peace
to a buffalo hunter
whose distracted gaze falls on
the colored tents
and the acrid smoke from the bonfires.
A crow flaps close on wings of woe.

IV

Fruits with an unpleasant
metallic taste are signs of
the Doleful Islands.
A ship is gently sinking
and the sailors are pulling
for a beach where a wild boar
is burying its prey. The sand
is blinding to the gods.

V

Cold air passes over
the hard shells
of the crustaceans.
A great shriek splits
the sky with its frozen
lightning flash of rage.
Like a gray carpet, they
descend, night and terror.

VI

The runaway carriage bolts
and a woman screams for help,
her clothing in disorder,
her hair loose in the wind.
The driver downs a huge
flagon of cider,
leaning unconcerned against
a marble torso.
Hedgehogs mark the road
with their long
nocturnal spines.

VII

A seaplane flies
over the jungle. There below

the missionaries wave
as they prepare for the wedding
of the chief. A whiff of cinnamon
spreads through the atmosphere
and on, to lose itself in
the fading drone of the plane.

VIII

A city walled in with vast stones
conceals the stiffened corpse of the queen
and the sweet, decaying flesh of her last
folly, an ice-cream seller,
his hair combed like a schoolgirl's.

IX

Venus emerges from the skimpy
crest of a palm.
In her right hand she holds
the fruit of a banana
with the peeled skin hanging down
like a soft, golden canopy.
Summer arrives
and a fisherman exchanges
a pound of clams
for a fencing mask.

The Wanderer Explains

I come from the North,
where they forge iron,
where they make locks and grills,
iron gates and inexhaustible arms,
where great bearskins cover walls and litters,
where the milk waits for a signal from the stars;

from the North, where every voice speaks an order,
where the sledges draw their breath under a sky
with no shadow of storm,
I am going eastward, toward warmer channels
of mud and clay,
and the patient, vegetal sleeplessness
fed by the immeasurable waters.
It's to the estuaries I'm finally going,
to the delta where the light rests, brooding on
the magnolias of death,
and the heat spreads across vast regions
in a dense siesta
lulled by the wings
of restless insects.
Even so, I would still yearn for
the leather workshops, the sparse sand,
the cold slithering through the dunes
where the glass sings
and the wind scourges
the ground and the grave-mounds,
blurring the tracks of the caravans.
I came from the North.
Ice annulled the labyrinths
where the sword obeys
the summons to its destiny.
I speak of traveling, not of resting places.
In the East, the moon broods over the region
that my hurt self reaches out to for relief
from a clutching dread, a dread that has no cure.

Acknowledgements

Editor's thanks to Jane Rose at the National Library of Scotland; the staff of the Scottish Poetry Library; Robin Hodge, who lent me his house; Stuart Kelly and Alan Taylor for their advice; and Michael McCreath for his timely help.